A Concise
User's Guide to
Windows 3.1

ALSO AVAILABLE
(By the same author)

A Concise User's Guide to Windows 3.1

by

Noel Kantaris

BERNARD BABANI (publishing) LTD.
THE GRAMPIANS
SHEPHERDS BUSH ROAD
LONDON W6 7NF
ENGLAND

PLEASE NOTE

Although every care has been taken with the production of this book to ensure that any projects, designs, modifications and/or programs, etc., contained herewith, operate in a correct and safe manner and also that any components specified are normally available in Great Britain, the Publishers and Author(s) do not accept responsibility in any way for the failure (including fault in design) of any project, design, modification or program to work correctly or to cause damage to any equipment that it may be connected to or used in conjunction with, or in respect of any other damage or injury that may be so caused, nor do the Publishers accept responsibility in any way for the failure to obtain specified components.

Notice is also given that if equipment that is still under warranty is modified in any way or used or connected with home-built equipment then that warranty may be void.

First Published - July 1992
Reprinted - December 1992
Reprinted - July 1993

British Library Cataloguing in Publication Data

Kantaris, Noel
    Concise User's Guide to Windows 3.1
    I. Title
    005.4

    ISBN 0 85934 325 1

Front cover illustration by Rachael A. Kantaris
Printed and Bound in Great Britain by Cox & Wyman Ltd, Reading

ABOUT THIS BOOK

This Concise User's Guide to Windows 3.1 was written to help the beginner. The material in the book is presented on the "what you need to know first, appears first" basis, although the underlying structure of the book is such that you don't have to start at the beginning and go right through to the end. The more experienced user can start from any section, as the sections have been designed to be self contained.

Windows is a Graphical User Interface (GUI) program, which not only acts as a graphical front-end to your PC's Disc Operating System (DOS), but also contains its own word processor, database, communications, and electronic calendar modules, to name but a few, all of which are examined in this book. Getting to grips with Windows cuts down the learning curve on other available packages specifically designed to run under the Windows environment.

For example, once you have learned to install printers and switch between them, you'll never again have any difficulty in doing the same thing from within other applications which run under Windows. Furthermore, learning to manipulate text in the Windows' Write module will lay very strong foundations on which to build expertise when you need to master a fully blown word processor with strong elements of desktop publishing.

The book was written with the busy person in mind. You don't need to read hundreds of pages to find out most there is to know about the subject, when a few pages can do the same thing quite adequately! Therefore, it is hoped that with the help of this small book, you will be able to get the most out of your computer, when using Windows, in terms of efficiency and productivity, and that you will be able to do it in the shortest, most effective and informative way.

ABOUT THE AUTHOR

Graduated in Electrical Engineering at Bristol University and after spending three years in the Electronics Industry in London, took up a Tutorship in Physics at the University of Queensland. Research interests in Ionospheric Physics, led to the degrees of M.E. in Electronics and Ph.D. in Physics. On return to the UK, he took up a Post-Doctoral Research Fellowship in Radio Physics at the University of Leicester, and in 1973 a Senior Lectureship in Engineering at The Camborne School of Mines, Cornwall, where since 1978 he has also assumed the responsibility of Head of Computing.

ACKNOWLEDGEMENTS

I would like to thank colleagues at the Camborne School of Mines for the helpful tips and suggestions which assisted me in the writing of this book.

TRADEMARKS

CONTENTS

1. PACKAGE OVERVIEW

Windows 3.1 is a Graphical User Interface (GUI) program, which acts as a graphical front end to the Disc Operating System (DOS). It simplifies all the DOS operations by converting the usual commands you have to type in the DOS command line (following the C:\> prompt), into pull-down menus which is the function of the Windows File Manager. The basic package includes its own word processor called Write, a graphics program called Paintbrush, a telecommunications program called Terminal, a monthly and daily electronic appointments program called Calendar, and a flat-file database called Cardfile. All these 'accessory' programs will be discussed separately as we progress through the book.

Unlike the 2.x versions of Windows, first version 3.0 and now version 3.1 have won the hearts of all sceptics to such graphical front-ends with their superior functionality. However, you must install the full Windows package to get full advantage of its new features and to access the applications running under its environment, as Windows 3.x does not support the Single Application Environment which used to come with certain Windows 2.x packages. One of the strengths of Windows 3.x lies in its ability to manage all other programs that run on your computer, whether these programs were specifically written for the Windows environment or not. Windows allows easy communication between such programs, but to what extend depends on the type of hardware at your disposal.

If the programs you want to use on your computer were specifically written to run under Windows, such as truly Wysiwyg (what-you-see-is-what-you-get) word processors, or superior spreadsheets which can incorporate worksheet tables with spreadsheet charts on the same screen display, then you only need to master Windows to be able to manage these other programs quite well, as Windows applications are written to look and feel substantially the same as the Windows program which controls their environment. This means, of course, that you can save a substantial amount of time by cutting down on the learning curve of each new program you intend to use.

Finally, Windows 3.1 caters for many new technological developments that have come about since Windows 3.0 was first released. These will be discussed shortly.

1

New Features

Some of the major enhancements Windows 3 has over earlier releases of the package include:

- A new SETUP program which makes installation very easy.

- A vastly improved and truly graphical interface using good looking icons.

- The ability to modify your system configuration without having to re-install Windows.

- The ability to organise files into logical groups, regardless of their physical location on your disc.

- The ability to multitask both Windows and standard DOS applications.

- The ability to record keyboard and mouse sequences with an in-built macro recorder.

- The ability to support the HP LaserJet and PostScript printers.

- Compatibility with a number of key networks.

Version 3.1 has additional advantages over version 3.0. These include:

- The ability to use scalable TrueType fonts that provide you with enough variety to meet practically all your printing needs.

- The ability to transfer and share information by Object Linking and Embedding (OLE). This is now available in applications such as Microsoft Excel, Ami Professional, and WordPerfect, in addition to the Windows applications Write, Paintbrush, Cardfile, and Sound Recorder.

- The ability to work with Multimedia, so that different kinds of media, including graphics, sound, animation, and video, can be incorporated into files and documents.

- The ability to start an application, or group of applications, by dragging and dropping the application's icon into the new 'startup' group.

- The inclusion of a new File Manager which displays on a split screen, both the directory list and the contents of the 'open' directory. A new 'drag and drop' feature makes it easier to move, copy, or print a file.

- The inclusion of the new NetWare network protocol and shell, making networking easier to install and use.

- The ability to run DOS applications much better with an improved level of support, including the capability to share file and code information with Windows applications.

Hardware Requirements

To install Windows 3.1 you need an IBM AT-compatible or PS/2 computer equipped with Intel's 80286, or 80386 (or higher), processor. Although Windows 3.0 can be installed on an IBM XT-compatible computer (equipped with an 8088 or 8086 processor), program execution is very slow indeed and only in the limited Windows 2 compatibility mode, known as 'Real' mode. Windows 3.1 does not support this mode.

Installing Windows 3.1 on an 80286 machine requires 6.0MB of hard disc space (9 MB is recommended), while installing it on an 80386 (or higher) processor machine, requires 8MB (10MB is recommended). These two different modes of running Windows depend on the type of processor your computer is using, as well as the amount of available Random Access Memory (RAM) in your computer. These are:

Standard mode   if you have an 80286 processor with 1MB or more of RAM, of which at least 256KB is extended memory,

Enhanced mode   if you have an 80386SX or higher processor with 2MB or more of RAM, of which at least 1MB is extended memory.

Although it is possible to operate Windows from the keyboard, the availability of a mouse is a must if you are going to benefit from the program's Graphical User Interface (GUI). After all, pointing and clicking (with the left mouse button) at an option on the screen to start an operation, or pointing and double-clicking at an icon to start a program, is a lot easier than having to learn several different key combinations. So if you can, install a mouse.

Installing Windows

Installing Windows on your computer's hard disc is made very easy with the use of the SETUP program, which even configures windows automatically to take advantage of the computer's hardware. You need to run the SETUP program because part of its job is to convert compressed Windows files from the distribution discs prior to copying them onto your hard disc.

However, before you start installing Windows, make sure you are not running any memory resident programs such as APPEND or GRAPHICS, to mention but two. If you have any entries in your **autoexec.bat** file that cause such programs to run, use the **Edit** screen editor and disable the relevant commands by adding the REM statement in front of them. Having done so, restart your computer by pressing the three key combination **Ctrl+Alt+Del** simultaneously.

To start installation, insert the Microsoft Windows distribution disc #1 into drive A:, log onto it by typing A: and type

SETUP

at the A:\> prompt. After a few seconds the following screen will be displayed.

```
Windows Setup
═══════════

    Welcome to Setup.

    The Setup program for Windows 3.1 prepares Windows
    to run on your computer.

        · To learn more about Windows Setup before continuing, press F1.

        · To set up Windows now, press ENTER.

        · To quit Setup without installing Windows, press F3.




ENTER=Continue  F3=Exit  F1=Help
```

On pressing <Enter> the program continues and offers you two alternative methods of installing itself; 'Express Setup', or 'Custom Setup', as shown overleaf.

```
Windows Setup
_____

    Windows provides two Setup methods:

    Express Setup (Recommended)
    Express Setup relies on Setup to make decisions,
    so setting up Windows is quick and easy.

      To use Express Setup, press ENTER.


    Custom Setup
    Custom Setup is for experienced computer users who
    want to control how Windows is set up. To use this Setup method,
    you should know how to use a mouse with Windows.

      To use Custom Setup, press C.

    For details about both Setup methods, press F1.


  ENTER=Express Setup  C=Custom Setup  F1=Help  F3=Exit
```

On pressing either <Enter> to select the 'Express Setup' option (recommended for most users and when upgrading from Windows 3.0), or <C> to select the 'Custom Setup' option (for experienced users only), the program continues and offers you the option of installing Windows in the

  C:\WINDOWS

directory as shown below.

```
Windows Setup
_____

    Setup has found a previous version of Microsoft Windows on your hard
    disk in the path shown below. It is recommended that you upgrade this
    previous version to Windows version 3.1.

      · To upgrade, press ENTER.

    If necessary, you can keep your older version of Windows and add
    Windows version 3.1 to your system. Press the BACKSPACE key to erase
    the path shown, and then type a new path for version 3.1.

      · When the correct path for Windows 3.1 is shown below, press ENTER.

     C:\WINDOWS

    Note: if you set up Windows version 3.1 in a new directory instead of
    upgrading, you will not maintain any of your desktop settings or any
    Program Manager groups and icons you set up. Also, you must make sure
    that only version 3.1 is listed in PATH in your AUTOEXEC.BAT file.


  ENTER=Continue  F1=Help  F3=Exit
```

On pressing <Enter>, the displayed directory is automatically created on the C: drive (if it does not already exist). Since most Windows applications also offer this default directory, you might as well accept it.

The program then detects your computer's processor and display, and if you have chosen the 'Express Setup' option, configures Windows to run with your system, and updates the necessary files. If you are upgrading from Windows 3.0, the 'Express Setup' option retains all your desktop settings and icon groupings. If, on the other hand, you have chosen the 'Custom Setup', the program presents you with information and asks for verification about your system, such as type of computer, monitor, mouse, keyboard, and language used, as shown below. In addition, you have control over the proposed changes to your **config.sys** and **autoexec.bat** files that are necessary to configure Windows to your system.

```
Windows Setup

    Setup has determined that your system includes the following hardware
    and software components. If your computer or network appears on the
    Hardware Compatibility List with an asterisk, press F1 for Help.

        Computer:          MS-DOS System
        Display:           VGA
        Mouse:             Microsoft, or IBM PS/2
        Keyboard:          Enhanced 101 or 102 key US and Non US keyboards
        Keyboard Layout:   US
        Language:          English (American)
        Network:           No Network Installed

        No Changes:        The above list matches my computer.

    If all the items in the list are correct, press ENTER to indicate
    "No Changes." If you want to change any item in the list, press the
    UP or DOWN ARROW key to move the highlight to the item you want to
    change. Then press ENTER to see alternatives for that item.

 ENTER=Continue  F1=Help  F3=Exit
```

Changing System Settings

To change an item in the list of the System Settings screen, move the highlighted cursor using the Up- or Down-arrow keys over the required item in the list and press <Enter> to reveal alternatives. For example, you might be using Windows in the UK and would like to change the 'Keyboard Layout' and 'Language' options from the displayed list. However, you don't have to change anything at this stage as both these entries can be changed at a later stage.

For the sake of completeness, and in order that you can find out easily how to do this later, we include here the exact procedure under the appropriate section. For the present, you could press <Enter> to accept the offered list.

To change any of the hardware settings at a later stage (after you have completed the Windows installation), point and double click at the **Windows Setup** icon of the Main menu (more about this later), then point and click at the **Options** option and select the **Change System Settings** sub-menu from which you can change the Display, Keyboard, Mouse, and Network options. To see alternative options, press the down-arrow button at the extreme right of the highlighted option, highlight the new hardware choice and press the **OK** button. To close the 'Change System Settings' window, double click on the top left button of the window (the one with the large minus sign).

From now on, the SETUP program uncompresses files from the distribution discs and copies them onto your hard disc. So that you know which file is being copied at any given time, its name appears on the bottom right-hand corner of your display. The first file to be copied onto your hard disc is the SETUP.EXE file. When another disc is required, the program will ask you to insert it in the A: drive.

Towards the end of disc #2, Windows tests itself and presents you with a foretaste of the graphical front-end it will be running under. This is done in the form of a graphics display containing some explanatory text followed by a dialogue box which lists choices that you can make. The topmost section of this graphics display is shown below.

In the case of the 'Express Setup' option, the program asks you to wait while it installs your printer, then it presents you with a dialogue box which asks you to give details of your name and company's name.

7

In the case of the 'Custom Setup' option, the dialogue box asks whether you would like to set up only Windows components you select, set up printers, and allow SETUP to search your hard disc in order to set up applications under Windows. In this case, it is a good idea to accept all three options by pointing and clicking at the **Continue** button. After all the options have been fulfilled, SETUP gives you the option of automatically making the necessary changes to your **config.sys** and **autoexec.bat** files, let you review the proposed changes before modifying these files, or let you make the modifications later.

If you don't get such a graphics display on your screen, then read the 'Troubleshooting' chapter in the Windows User's Guide for possible solution to your problem, before re-installing Windows again.

Installing a Printer:

When you choose to install a printer, Windows presents you with a 'List of Printers' from which you can choose the particular printer or printers you want to use, as shown below.

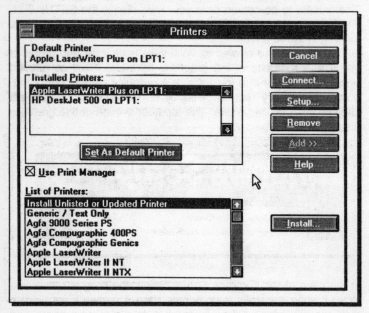

Here, two printer drivers were installed; a PostScript Apple Laser Writer Plus as the 'default' printer, and configured for output via the parallel port LPT1, and the HP DeskJet 500 printer, configured to print to a disc file. The choice of installing an additional printer driver could be dependent on whether such a printer was available to you at, say, your office on a shared basis. This would allow the preparation of documents incorporating fonts and styles, not available on the printer connected to your system, to be saved on disc and printed later on a printer which supports such enhancements and perhaps produces better output.

Each time you choose to install a different printer, Windows will ask you to insert a particular disc in the A: drive, so that the appropriate printer driver (a file containing the instructions Windows needs to control that printer) is copied to your computer's hard disc. Adding printers can be done at a later stage by double clicking at the **Control Panel** icon of the Main group of applications (see end of chapter), then double clicking at the **Printers** icon, and pressing the **A̲dd Printer** button.

Setting Up Applications:
The next step in the Windows SETUP is the search by the program of your computer's hard disc(s) to allow you to set up applications to run under Windows. Some of these applications might be standard DOS controlled applications, others might have been written specifically to run under Windows. On execution of this choice, the screen shown below is displayed.

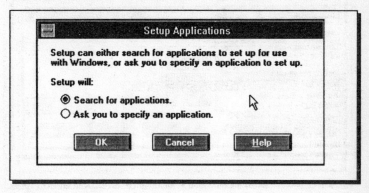

9

Again, adding applications to Windows can be done at a later stage (you will have to do this every time you add a new application you want to run in the Windows environment) by double-clicking at the **Windows Setup** icon of the Main group of applications, then clicking at the **Options**, and selecting **Set Up Applications** option from the revealed sub-menu.

If you select the 'Search for applications' option, SETUP displays a further dialogue box, as shown below.

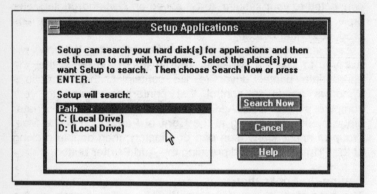

To select other than the default 'Path' search, point and click at the specific hard drive you want to search and press the **Search Now** button. After a short while, the following display appears on your screen:

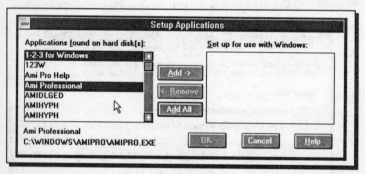

Use the mouse pointer to point and click at applications you would like to run under Windows. This highlights the application and at the same time produces an icon, to be used in conjunction with that application, at the bottom of the list, and also specifies the full path of the said application, which can be useful if you have two different versions of an application. You can look at more applications on the list by clicking at the down-arrow at the bottom of the scroll bar which appears to the right of the list of named applications.

Once you have highlighted all the applications you would like to add to Windows, press the **Add ->** button. The selected applications are now transferred to the right-hand side of the display, as shown below.

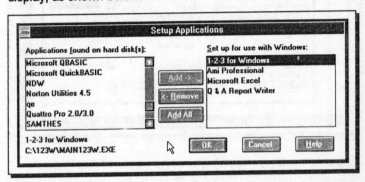

You can press the **OK** button to have these applications set up for use with Windows, or you can highlight one or more and then press the **<- Remove** button before pressing the **OK** button. Adding a program means including in a Windows window its name and an in-built identifying icon. To achieve the latter, Windows might ask you to insert disc #7 in the A: drive so that it can load the particular icon of a selected application.

Read On-line Documents:
Lastly, SETUP displays the on-line documentation which is held in 3 files with the extension **.txt**. These are loaded automatically on the 'Notepad' so that you can read them. They contain useful advice which you might like to read, particularly if you have any problems with getting Windows to run properly. You don't have to read the on-line documentation files right now, as these are available to you at any time.

To read this documentation later, point and double click at the Notepad icon of the Accessories group of applications, then select the **File, Open** command which causes the screen shown below to be displayed:

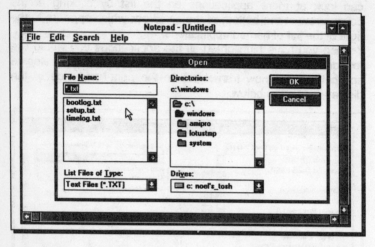

Of these, the file **setup.txt** is perhaps worth reading in detail.

There are other on-line documents that are copied to your hard disc, but which have the **.wri** extension. They are best read by using 'Windows Write'. Of the offered documents, perhaps the **readme.wri** file is worth looking at, as it contains information updated after the user's guide was printed.

Once you have read the on-line documentation, you can exit from the Notepad by following the steps detailed in the 'Instructions' box.

Completing Installation

If you are upgrading Windows, all that remains in order to exit SETUP is to select the **Restart Windows** option from the next display which forces the program to restart by resetting your system to the new parameters changed during set up.

If, on the other hand, you are installing Windows with the 'Custom Setup' option, you will need to look into some final points to complete installation. For example, you need to specify the country, language and keyboard layout of your system, because SETUP doesn't always make the correct choice.

The other option on this last SETUP display allows you to **Return to DOS** without taking any further steps. If you choose this option and want to continue with what follows, then you will need to restart Windows by typing **win** at the DOS prompt (more about this later).

To specify the country, language and keyboard layout of your system, double click at the **Control Panel** icon of the Main group of applications (see end of chapter), then double click at the **International** icon, and change the displayed settings to what is shown in the display below (if you are a UK user that is, and agree with the various date and time formats).

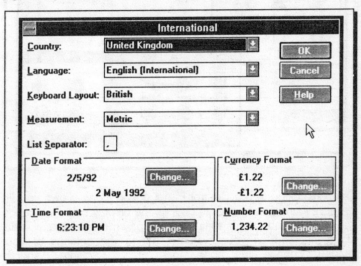

For alternative options from those displayed, select the required field in the dialogue box and click on the down-arrow button at the extreme right of it, and highlight a new choice. After changing all the default options, press the **OK** button.

To change any of the hardware settings, double click at the **Windows Setup** icon of the Main group of applications, then click at the **Options** and select the **Change System Settings** sub-menu from which you can change the 'Display', 'Keyboard', 'Mouse', and 'Network' options.

The Control Panel

The Windows Control Panel provides a quick and easy way to change the hardware and software settings of your system. For the sake of completeness we describe its use at this point.

To access the Control Panel, double-click at its icon on the Main group of applications, which opens the following window from which the various Control Panel options can be accessed:

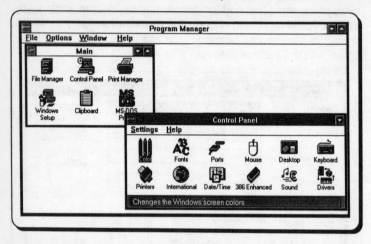

Double-clicking at the Control Panel option icons allows you (in order of icon appearance) to change the display colours, change the display and printer fonts, specify parameters for any serial ports installed on your system, change the settings of your mouse, change the appearance of your display, specify resources allocation when running in 386 mode, install and configure your printer(s), specify international settings, such as the formatting of numbers and dates, change the keyboard repeat rate, change the date and time of your system, and specify whether Windows should beep when it detects an error.

2. WORKING WITH WINDOWS

Starting Windows

To start Windows you need only type the word **win** at the C:\> prompt. When the program is loaded, the following display appears on your screen.

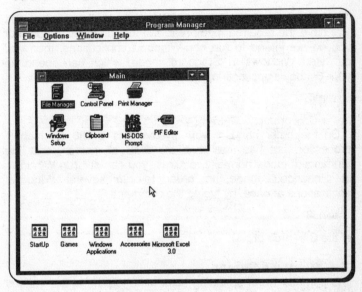

This easy way of starting up the program (you don't need to change to the directory where you installed Windows) was arranged by SETUP when you allowed it to modify the contents of your system's **autoexec.bat** file, by the addition of the \WINDOWS directory into the PATH command. Indeed, it is imperative that the \WINDOWS directory is part of the PATH, otherwise Windows will not work. (Don't try to start the program with a batch file - it won't work properly).

If you have any problems in loading Windows or running the program in a satisfactory manner, first refer to the documentation that comes with the package to make sure you have interpreted correctly the advice given. If things don't improve, read Appendix A (entitled 'Fine Tuning Windows') before you call Microsoft's customer service.

Starting Windows with Switches:
Windows can be forced to start in other than the default mode (provided your hardware supports it) by appending one of two special switches to the **win** command. These are:

/S   to force Windows to start in 286 Standard mode, or
/3   to force Windows to start in 386 Enhanced mode.

Thus, if your system has a 386SX (or higher) processor and you have the required memory to run in 'Enhanced' mode, but you do not intend to run non-Windows applications, then you can start Windows in 'Standard' mode, which can speed up your Windows application, by typing the command

 win /S

at the C:\> prompt.
 On the other hand, if your system has a 386 (or higher) processor, but has less than the 2MB of memory that the 'Enhanced' mode normally requires, you can still run Windows in 'Enhanced' mode, in order to run several Windows applications at once, by typing the command

 win /3

at the C:\> prompt.

The Windows Screen
It is perhaps worth spending some time looking at the various parts that make up the Windows screen - we use the word 'Windows' to refer to the whole environment, while the word 'windows' refers to application or document windows. There are two types of windows that can appear on your screen; 'applications' windows which contain running applications, and 'document' windows which appear with applications that can open more than one document (we will see an example of this shortly), but share the application window's menu.
 Windows makes use of three types of icons; 'application icons' which only appear at the bottom of your screen after you choose to minimise that application, 'document icons' which appear at the bottom of the application window when you minimise that document (for example, the Accessories and Games icons in the previous screen dump), and 'program icons' which are the icons that appear within a group window in the

Program Manager application (for example, those in the Main group of the previous screen dump).

The icons within the Main group have the following function:

Program icon	Function
File Manager	Performs file related operations
Control Panel	Changes system configuration
Print Manager	Manages printing operations
Windows Setup	Calls SETUP to add applications
Clipboard	Transfers data between windows
MS-DOS Prompt	Allows temporary exit to DOS
PIF Editor	Allows you to edit DOS applications start-up files.

The document icons which appear at the bottom of the Program Manager window have the following function:

Document icon	Function
Accessories	Contains the applications Write, Paintbrush, Terminal, Notepad, Recorder, Cardfile, Calendar, Calculator, Clock, Object Packager, Media Player, Sound Recorder, and Character Map.
Games	Contains three games, namely, Reversi, Solitaire, and Minesweeper.
Windows Applications	Contains Windows applications SETUP found on your hard disc during installation.
Non-Windows Applications	Contains any standard DOS applications that SETUP incorporated into the Windows environment during installation.

Parts of a Window:

Each application and some documents you choose to work with open and use separate windows to run in. In order to illustrate the various parts of the Windows screen, we chose to run the Write program which is to be found within the Accessories group of programs. If you would like to see the same thing on your screen, first double-click the Accessories document icon and then double-click on the Write application icon.

Although every window has some common elements, not all windows use all of these elements.

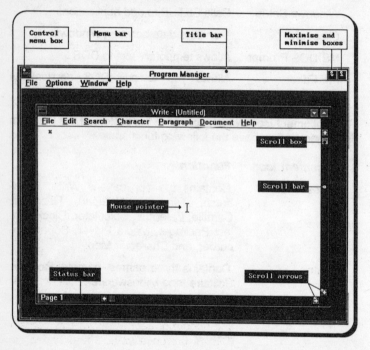

Note that the applications window (Write), which in this case displays an empty (and [Untitled]) sheet, has a solid 'Title bar', indicating that it is the active applications window. Although multiple windows can be displayed simultaneously, you can only enter data into the active window (displayed at the top). Title bars of nonactive windows appear a lighter shade than that of the active one.

The Windows screen is subdivided into several areas which have the following function:

Area	Function
Control menu box	Clicking on this box, which is located in the upper-left corner of each window, displays the pull-down Control menu through which the active document window is controlled. It includes commands for resizing, moving, maximising, minimising, switching to another task, and closing the window
Title bar	The bar at the top of a window. The actual title depends on the type of Windows application
Menu bar	The bar below the title bar which allows you to choose from several menu options. Clicking on a menu item displays the pull-down menu associated with that item. The specific options listed in the Menu bar depend on the application running in the window
Minimise box	The button you point to and click to store an application as a small symbol at the bottom of the screen
Maximise box	The button you point to and click to fill the screen with the active window. When that happens, the Maximise button changes to a Restore (vertical double-headed) arrow which can be used to restore the window to its former size
Scroll bars	The areas on the screen (extreme right and bottom of each window) that contain a scroll box in a vertical and horizontal bar. Clicking on these bars allows you to see parts of a document that might not be visible in that size window
Scroll arrows	The arrowheads at each end of each scroll bar at which you can click to scroll the screen up and down one line, or left and right one character, at a time

| Status bar | The area at the lower-left corner of a window in which the current program status and present process is displayed |
| Mouse pointer | In this particular shape it is called a 'selection' cursor. It shows where you are in a particular document and marks the place where text or graphics appears when you start typing or drawing. |

The Menu Bar Options:

Each window's menu bar option has associated with it a pull-down sub-menu, with the Control menu common to all applications. To activate the menu of a window, either press the <Alt> key, which causes the first option of the menu (in this case **File**) to be highlighted, then use the right and left arrow keys to highlight any of the options in the menu, or use the mouse to point to an option. Pressing either the <Enter> key, or the left mouse button, reveals the pull-down sub-menu of the highlighted menu option. The sub-menu of the **File** option of the maximised Program Manager's window, is shown below.

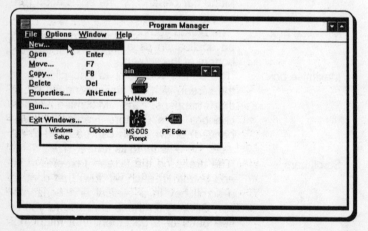

Menu options can also be activated directly by pressing the <Alt> key followed by the underlined letter of the required option. Thus pressing **Alt+F**, causes the pull-down sub-menu of the **File** to be displayed. You can use the up and down arrow keys to move the highlighted bar up and down a sub-menu, or the right and left arrow keys to move along the options in the menu bar. Pressing the <Enter> key selects the highlighted option or executes the highlighted command. Pressing the <Esc> key once, closes the pull-down sub-menu, while pressing the <Esc> key for a second time, closes the menu system.

Each item on the menu bar offers the following options:

File   Produces a pull-down menu of mainly file related tasks, such as creating a 'new' program group, 'open' Clipboard, 'move' a program item from one program group to another, 'copy' a program item from one program group to another, 'delete' a highlighted program item from the active window, display the 'properties' of a program item and allow you to change its icon, 'run' a program by entering its name from the keyboard, and 'exit Windows'.

Options   Selecting 'auto arrange' allows Windows to arrange icons automatically within the active window, while selecting 'minimize on use' minimises the Program Manager when a program is run. Once selected, such an option show a checkmark against its name. Selecting such an option once more, removes the checkmark and toggles the option off.

Window   Allows you to display multiple windows on your screen in 'cascade' or 'tile' form, or 'arrange icons' within an active window in a pre-determined spacing. The options numbered 1-5 on this sub-menu (they could be less in your case) identify the program groups in the Window environment installed by SETUP. If you create a new program group, another numbered option is added to the sub-menu. A checkmark against a number indicates that the corresponding option is the currently active window.

Help   Activates the help window and displays an 'index' of help or offers help on selected topics.

Dialogue Boxes:
Three periods after a sub-menu option or command, means that a dialogue box will open when the option or command is selected. A dialogue box is used for the insertion of additional information, such as the name of a file.

To see a couple of dialogue boxes, point and click (once) on the File Manager icon to highlight it, press **Alt+F**, and select the **Properties**. The Program Item Properties dialogue box appears on the screen, and when you press the **Change Icon** button, the Selection dialogue box is revealed. As each dialogue box was displayed on screen, it was moved slightly (by pointing at its Title bar, pressing the left mouse button and while keeping it pressed, dragging it to a new position) to produce the following display:

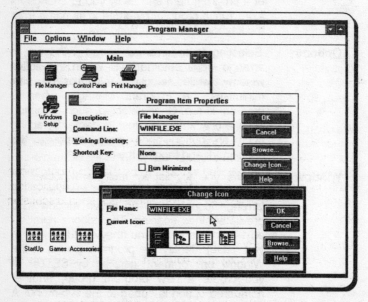

When a dialogue box opens, the <Tab> key can be used to move the cursor from one field to another (Shift+<Tab> moves the cursor backwards) or alternatively you can move directly to a desired field by holding the <Alt> key down and pressing the underlined letter in the field name. Within a group of options you can use the arrow keys to move from one option to another.

Having selected an option or typed in information, you must press a command button such as the **OK** or **Cancel** button, or choose from additional options. To select the **OK** button with the mouse, simply point and click, while with the keyboard, you must first press the <Tab> key until the dotted rectangle moves to the required button, and then press the <Enter> key.

Some dialogue boxes contain List boxes which show a column of available choices. If there are more choices than can be seen in the area provided, use the scroll bars to reveal them. To select a single item from a List box, either double-click the item, or use the arrow keys to highlight the item and press <Enter>. Other dialogue boxes contain Option buttons with a list of mutually exclusive items. The default choice is marked with a black dot against its name, while unavailable options are dimmed. Another type of dialogue box contains Check boxes which offer a list of options you can switch on or off. Selected options show a cross in the box against the option name.

To cancel a dialogue box, either press the **Cancel** button, or press the <Esc> key. Pressing the <Esc> key in succession, closes one dialogue box at a time, and eventually aborts the menu option.

Manipulating Windows

Windows allows the display of multiple application windows. It is conceivable that at some stage you would like to manipulate these windows, by selecting which is to be the active one, move them so that you can see all the relevant parts of an application, or indeed size such windows. What follows is a short discussion on how to manipulate windows.

Changing the Active Window:

To select the active window amongst those displayed on the screen, point to it and click the left mouse button, or select the **W**indow option of the main menu and select the appropriate number of the window you want to make the active one.

Moving Windows, Dialogue Boxes, and Icons:

When you have multiple windows or dialogue boxes on the screen, you might want to move a particular one to a different part of the screen. Moving windows and dialogue boxes can be achieved with either the mouse or the keyboard.

To move a window, a dialogue box, or an icon with the mouse, point to the title bar or icon and drag it (press the left button and keep it pressed while moving the mouse) until the shadow border is where you would like it to be. Then release the mouse button to fix it into its new position.

To move an application window, a dialogue box, or an icon with the keyboard, press **Alt+<Spacebar>** to reveal the Application Control menu, or **Alt+<->** to reveal the Document Control menu. Then, press **m** to select <u>**M**</u>ove which causes a four-headed arrow to appear in the title bar and use the arrow keys to move the shadow border of the window to the required place. Press <Enter> to fix the window to its new position or <Esc> to cancel relocation.

Sizing a Window:
You can change the size of a window with either the mouse or the keyboard.

To size an active window with the mouse, move the window so that the side you want to change is visible, then move the mouse pointer to the edge of the window or corner so that it changes to a two-headed arrow, then drag the two-headed arrow in the direction you want that side or corner to move. Continue dragging until the shadow border is the size you require, then release the mouse button.

To size with the keyboard, press either **Alt+<Spacebar>** or **Alt+<->** to reveal the Application Control menu or the Document Control menu, then press **s** to select <u>**S**</u>ize which causes a four-headed arrow to appear. Now press the arrow key that corresponds to the edge you want to move, or if a corner, press the two arrow keys (one after the other) corresponding to the particular corner, which causes the pointer to change to a two-headed arrow. Press an appropriate arrow key in the direction you want that side or corner to move and continue to do so until the shadow border is the size you require, then press <Enter> to fix the new window size.

Minimising and Maximising Windows:
Application windows can be minimised into short icons at the bottom of the screen, temporarily freeing screen space. This can be done by either using the mouse to click at the 'Minimise' button (the downward arrow in the upper-right corner of the

24

window), or by pressing **Alt+<Spacebar>** or **Alt+<->** to reveal the Application Control menu or the Document Control menu, and selecting **n** for **Minimize**.

To maximise a window so that it fills the entire screen, either click on the 'maximise' button (the upward arrow in the upper-right corner of the window), or press **Alt+<Spacebar>** or **Alt+<->** to display the Application Control menu or the Document Control menu, and select **x** for **Maximize**.

An application which has been minimised or maximised can be returned to its original size and position on the screen by either double clicking on its icon to expand it to a window, or clicking on the double-headed button in the upper-right corner of the maximised window to reduce it to its former size. With the keyboard, press **Alt+<Spacebar>** to display the Application Control menu, or **Alt+<->** to display the Document Control menu, and select **r** for **Restore**.

Closing a Window

An application or document window can be closed at any time to save screen space and memory. To close a window either double click on the Control menu button (the large hyphen in the upper-left corner of the window, or press **Alt+<->** and select **c** for **Close** from the Control menu.

If you have made any changes to a document since the last time you saved it, Windows will warn you with the appearance of a dialogue box asking confirmation prior to closing it.

If you want to end a task, then activate the Control menu and select the **Switch To** option, which causes the following dialogue box to be displayed:

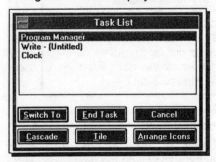

Both the Write and the Clock programs listed in the Task List opposite are in the Accessories group of programs. To obtain the same display as the one shown here, first double-click at the Accessories icon then double-click at the Write icon and minimise it, then repeat with the Clock icon.

25

To end a task, highlight its name in the Task List, then press the **End Task** button. As you can see from the other available options in the dialogue box, you can 'switch to' a different task, and can even display the windows of the listed tasks in 'cascade' or 'tile' form on your screen.

Windows Display Arrangement

The default layout of multiple windows on display on your computer's screen is in 'cascade' form - that is, overlapping one another, with each newly opened window being located slightly below and to the right of the previous one.

The option **Window** on the menu bar of Program Manager allows you the choice of having multiple windows automatically displayed in either 'cascade' or 'tile' form, or 'arrange icons' within an active window in a predetermined spacing. Which way you choose to dispay multiple windows is a matter of balance between personal preference and the type of work you are doing at the time.

As an illustration, the cascade type of display arrangement is shown below for the applications of 'Games', 'Windows Applications', 'Main', and 'Accessories'.

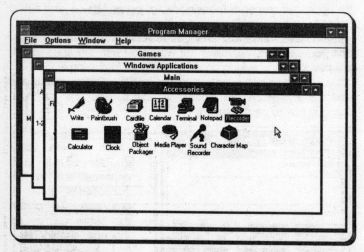

The same application windows will arrange themselves automatically in the display form shown on the next page, when the 'Tile' option is selected.

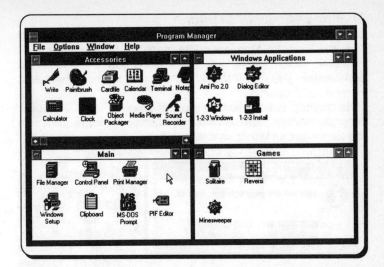

Finally, you can size the various windows manually and place them precisely where you want them on your screen to emulate a desk-top - you can even have a clock showing you the time! Try arranging the various windows as shown below:

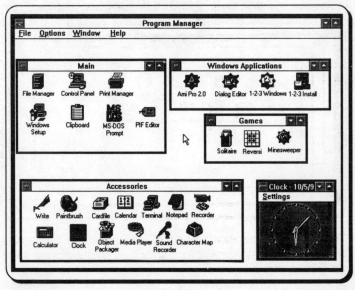

Ending a Windows Session

To end a Windows session, select the **Exit Windows** command from the Program Manager's **File** menu, or the Control menu. However, before doing so, make sure you first close the applications you are running so as not to lose the latest changes to your work.

No matter which method you choose to quit Windows, Program Manager always asks you to confirm your request with the following Exit Windows dialogue box:

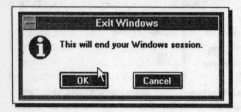

By default, the **Save Settings on Exit** choice, in the **Options** sub-menu of the Program Manager's window, is set to cause Windows to save the current display layout. Thus, the next time you start Windows, your desktop display will look the same as the last time you used the program. If you don't want to save the current display layout, then select **Options** from the Program Manager's menu and click at the **Save Settings on Exit** option to remove the tick mark against this sub-menu choice. From now on, this becomes the new default state for the Exit Windows dialogue box, until you decide to change it again.

3. THE THREE MANAGERS

Program Manager

The central and essential element in the Windows operation is Program Manager; it runs whenever you start Windows and continues to do so until you exit Windows. Other programs can be started from within Program Manager simply by double clicking at their icons. While other programs run, Program Manager continues to run in the background or as a minimised icon on your screen, euphemistically called the 'desktop'.

Program Manager allows you to organise your disc files in logical groups, irrespective of their physical location on the disc; something that DOS does not allow you to do. For example, when you first start Windows, Program Manager automatically opens the Main window which contains a certain group of applications. Other applications have been gathered together automatically by SETUP and put into the Accessories group, while others have been put into the Games group.

Program Manager not only allows you to regroup applications in your preferred way, but also to make up new application groups with the added convenience of allowing you to include the same application in more than one program group. As an illustration, let us create a new program group, called Utilities, in which we will gather all the useful programs we might need to help us make our system more efficient.

Creating a New Program Group:

To create a new program group, use the Program Manager's **File, New** command which displays the following dialogue box:

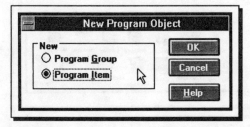

To create a new group, rather than add an item to an existing group, click at the Program Group option of the New Program Object dialogue box and press the **OK** button. This causes the Program Group Properties dialogue box to be displayed, as shown overleaf:

Enter the name 'Utilities' in the Description field which will be the name displayed in the title bar of the new group. Pressing <Enter>, will display a new window bearing the name 'Utilities'.

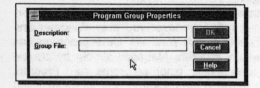

Leave the Group File field empty (even though you have the option to type in a different name for the group), because Windows normally assigns it the name you typed in the Description field with the extension .GRP in order to be able to find later what programs you have assigned to this group.

To copy a program to the Utilities group window, you must first open the group window where the program you want to copy resides; in our example, the Accessories group. Do this and size both group windows so they are visible on you screen.

A Program application can be copied with the mouse by pressing the **Ctrl** key and while keeping it pressed, dragging the application icon to the desired position within the Utilities window. Releasing the mouse button (and the **Ctrl** key) places a copy of the desired program in the new group window. With the keyboard, use the **File, Copy** command. If you have copied an application you did not mean to copy, then erase it from its new position by first highlighting it, and then either pressing the <Del> key, or using the **File, Delete** command. Now copy the three applications shown below to the Utilities window.

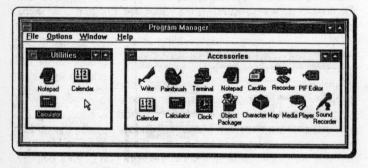

A program application can be moved from one group to another, by either dragging its icon to the new group window or using the **File, Move** command. Try moving the Clock from the Accessories to the Utilities and back again.

It is perhaps worth emphasising that by copying or moving an application to another group of programs, you are not in fact producing more copies of the program on your disc or changing the place where your program resides on your disc. You are simply regrouping programs is a logical rather than physical way.

Adding Files to a Program Group:
Sometimes you might find it useful to locate a program file that resides on your disc, but is not contained in any of the program groups available to you under Program Manager, and add it to one of them. Such a program file could be one that you have inadvertently deleted from a program group, or one that was never there in the first place.

To accomplish our task we need to use File Manager from the Main group of applications to locate such a program file, which typically uses the .COM, .EXE, .BAT, or .PIF file extension, and drag it to a group within Program Manager. File Manager is a powerful tool that can help with the organisation of files and directories on your disc, and as such will be dealt with in some detail later. For the moment we will simply use it.

There is a program available within the Windows' \SYSTEM subdirectory called **sysedit.exe** which allows you to view and edit the four main system files, namely the **config.sys** and **autoexec.bat,** to be found in the root directory of the C: drive, and the **win.ini** and **system.ini** files, to be found in the \WINDOWS directory. Incorporating this program within the Utilities group, could make it easier for you to use it (to fine tune Windows, as explained in Appendix A).

First, close all application windows except for the Main and Utilities groups (closed applications appear as small icons at the bottom of the Program Manager window). Next, drag the right edge of the Program Manager window to near the middle of your display, then point and double click on the File Manager icon and size its window so it fits in the right half of your display. Now, point and click on the \WINDOWS directory, then click on the SYSTEM subdirectory and scroll to the right until you locate

the SYSEDIT.EXE file and drag its icon into the Utilities group
window, as shown below:

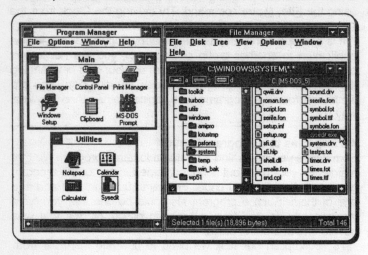

Finally, close the File Manager window and re-size the Program
Manager window to fill your screen. If you now point and double
click on the Sysedit icon, you get the System Configuration
Editor displaying all four system files, as shown below:

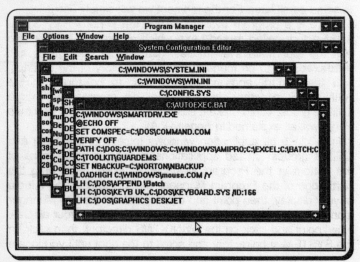

These files can be edited, by first making the relevant window active, and then saved by selecting the **File, Save** command.

Changing a Group's Properties:
To change the description of an individual item within a group, select the icon of the item and use the **File, Properties** command, while to change the description of a whole group of programs, first minimise the group, then select the group icon and use the **File, Properties** command. Limit such descriptions to less than 15 characters long, otherwise they will overlap, unless you use the Control Panel's Desktop module to increase the Icon Spacing, although this changes the spacing for *all* icon labels which decreases the number you can display at once.

With Windows 3.1, you can force a title to appear on two lines provided its name is made up of two words and the total length (including the space between the words) is more than 13 characters long. To illustrate the point, highlight the 'Character Map' icon within the Asseccories group (its description appears on a single line), then select the **File, Properties** option from the Program Manager's menu which displays the following dialogue box:

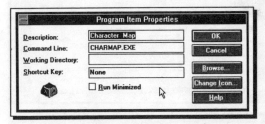

To see the title wrap to a second line, add a space between the two words describing the item, so that its length is now 14 characters. On pressing the **OK** button, the description of this item now appears on two lines.

To delete an individual item from within a group, select the item icon and use the **File, Delete** command while to delete a whole group of programs, first minimise the group, then select the group icon and use the **File, Delete** command. In both cases you will be prompted with an 'Are you sure' dialogue box, before the command is executed.

File Manager

To start File Manager, double-click at its icon which is the first one within the Main group of applications. File Manager, as well as Program Manager, are new to Windows 3, with the File Manager being much improved in version 3.1.

On starting File Manager its split window fills the screen with the 'directory tree' appearing on the left, and the 'lists of files' on the right. The appearance of the directory tree will depend on which **T**ree sub-menu options you have selected from the File Manager's menu bar. For example, selecting **C**ollapse Branch and **I**ndicate Expandable Branches, displays the following screen:

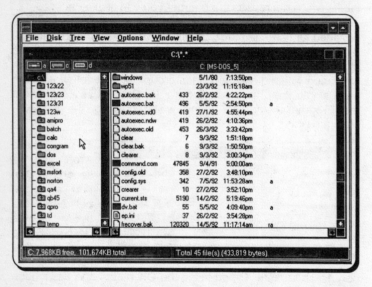

Your system will display different directories than the ones shown here, as it is bound to be structured differently. Nonetheless the 'root' directory, indicated by the back-slash sign (\), of a particular drive, is the main directory under which a number of directories can be created. In turn, each directory can have its own subdirectories, thus allowing you to keep data of similar applications, such as word processor documents or spreadsheet work-files, together in their respective sub-directories. File Manager helps you to organise your files and disc directories.

The Directory Tree:

From the directory tree you can list files within individual directories, or change the logged disc drive. Directories which are marked with a plus sign (+), contain subdirectories. Whether subdirectories appear collapsed and their presence is indicated with a plus sign (+), depends on the selections made within the **Tree** options from the File Manager's menu bar, as discussed earlier. Clicking once at such a collapsed icon, opens it up to reveal the subdirectories under it. Such subdirectories are shown below for the case of the WINDOWS directory.

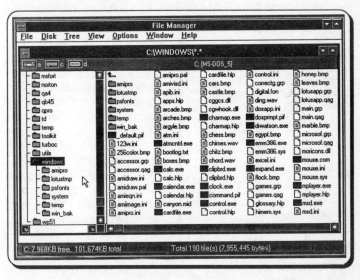

When subdirectories are displayed, the icon of the parent directory appears like an open file (as the one above) and, depending on the selections made within the **Tree** sub-menu, might also acquire a minus sign (–), indicating that it can be collapsed.

The right-hand side of the display is automatically displayed when you select a given directory from the directory tree. The title bar of this window is C:\WINDOWS*.*, indicating that all the files, including subdirectories, are listed. You can change the information shown in a directory window by using the **View** commands from the File Manager's menu bar.

For example, you could display information on the size of files and the date and time such files were created or last changed, by selecting the **All File Details** option of the **View** command. Such information can be used to find the latest version of a file amongst files with similar names. Note, however, that in the case of directories the size column is not displayed.

The File Manager Commands:

The File Command - The first of six commands (not counting **Help**) on the File Manager's menu bar, is **File**. Clicking on this command (or pressing Alt+F) displays its sub-menu, as follows:

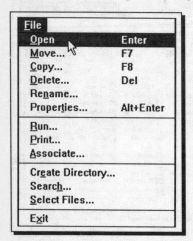

To illustrate how these commands can be used, first create a temporary directory, then search the hard disc for certain files, select some of these and copy them to the temporary directory. We will eventually discuss ways of deleting these files from the temporary directory, including the removal of the created directory itself. So, don't worry, the contents of your hard disc will not be changed.

To create a new directory, select 'Create Directory** from the sub-menu of **File** and type a name for it, say FILEBIN1, in the **N**ame field of the displayed 'Create Directory' dialogue box. On pressing the **OK** button the directory is created and is displayed in the correct alphabetical sequence in the directory tree.

To search a directory, say WINDOWS, for specific files, say those with the **.EXE** extension, highlight the WINDOWS directory on the directory tree, then select the **Search** option from the **File** sub-menu and type the information you want to search for, in this case *.EXE. Make sure to remove the cross from the 'Search All Subdirectories' box, before pressing the **OK** button, otherwise File Manager will find all the executable files on your hard disc, which can be rather a lot.

36

The names of the found files are then displayed in a 'Search Results' window as follows:

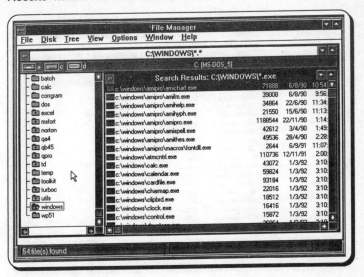

To select a single file to copy, point to it with the mouse and click once to highlight it. If you want to copy a group of contiguous files, then press the <Shift> key and while keeping it pressed select the files at the start and end of the block which results in all files in between to be selected. If you want to copy two separate blocks of files, press both the <Ctrl> and the <Shift> key at the same time and while keeping them pressed, select the files at the start and end of the first block, then release the <Shift> key (but keep the <Ctrl> key pressed) and select the first file of the second block, after which, press again the <Shift> key and select the last file of the second block.

To copy all the files in the 'Search Results' window to the FILEBIN1 directory, choose the **Select Files** option from the **File** sub-menu, accept the default *.* by pressing the **Select** button of the revealed dialogue box, then choose the **File, Copy** command. Next, type the destination directory (it could be another disc) in the displayed 'Copy To' dialogue box - in our case this is C:\FILEBIN1 - before pressing the **OK** button. When all the files have been copied return to the directory tree window and click on the FILEBIN1 directory icon.

The copied files are now displayed in a separate window with the title 'C:\FILEBIN1*.*', as shown below:

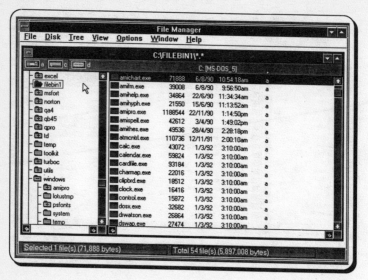

Before you go on, make sure you have created the FILEBIN1 directory and have copied into it the suggested files. What we are about to demonstrate is how to move files from one directory to another, and eventually, how to delete groups of files. Obviously such operations can only be demonstrated on files and directories which do not matter.

To move files from one directory into another, you mark the files you want to move and use the **File, Move** command. But first, let us create another directory - call it FILEBIN2. Since the current directory is C:\FILEBIN1, using the **File, Create Directory** command creates the new directory as a subdirectory of FILEBIN1. Now highlight the seven files in C:\FILEBIN1 whose names start with the letter C and then move them into the C:\FILEBIN1\FILEBIN2 directory. On executing the command, the seven files are moved from the original to the destination directory.

You can now safely delete a directory and its contents by first highlighting its name, and then using the **File, Delete** command. You will be asked for confirmation in a Delete dialogue box. Try deleting the FILEBIN2 subdirectory.

You can rename a directory, even though it contains files by selecting the **File, Rename** command. Try renaming FILEBIN1 to FILEBIN. Finally, to delete FILEBIN and all its contents might take some time if the 'Confirm On File Delete' option in the 'Confirmation' dialogue box of the **Options, Confirmation** command, was crossed. In the following dialogue box the cross has been removed from the **File Delete** box which allows you to automatically delete files without individual confirmation.

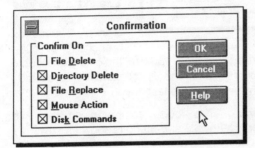

This, however, is as dangerous as the DOS command 'del *.*', so be *very* careful when using it on original files and directories. You will be asked only once if you mean what you say!

If you ever require the ability to view simultaneously the contents of two different directories or disc drives, simply double-click the drive icon to open an additional window for that drive, then select the **Window, Tile** command from the File Manager's menu bar to display both screens at the same time.

The Disc Command - The second command on the File Manager's menu bar allows you to perform several different types of operations on floppy discs, as shown on the following **Disk** command's sub-menu:

You can 'Copy a Disc' on to another, give a disc a 'Label', 'Format' a disc (advisable for only new discs, as it wipes the disc clean of all data), 'Make a System Disc' by copying on to it the system files, so that you can boot (start) your computer from that disc, or 'Select a Drive', including the selection or deselection of a network drive.

The Tree Command - The third command on the File Manager's menu bar is **T̲ree**. Its sub-menu is as follows:

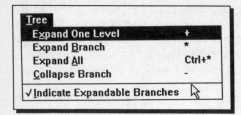

From here you can control what you see on your directory tree. For example, you can 'Expand a tree one level', 'Expand a branch', 'Expand all branches', or 'Col-lapse a branch'. At the same time, you can 'Indicate expandable branches' with the plus (+) sign and all collapsable branches by the minus (–) sign, by selecting the last option.

The View Command - The fourth command on the File Manager's menu bar is **V̲iew**. Its sub-menu is shown below:

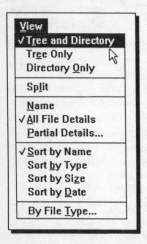

Most of these options are self-explanatory. You can use the **V̲iew, All File Details** option to see the file attributes in a directory window. The letters A, H, R, and S are used in the listing against a filename to indicate 'Archive', 'Hidden', 'Read Only', and 'System' files, respect-ively. Having found out what type of files you are dealing with, you can then change their attributes.

To change such file attributes, first select the file, then use the **F̲ile, Proper̲ties** command, which causes the 'File Properties' dialogue box to appear on your screen so that you can select or clear the appropriate check boxes.

Most of the other commands in the sub-menus of the File Manager's menu bar, are self-explanatory, therefore we will not pursue this discussion any further.

Starting Applications from File Manager:

You can start an application from the File Manager simply by locating its .EXE, .COM, .BAT, or .PIF file in the application's directory and double-click the filename.

For example, within the WINDOWS directory, you can recognise filenames such as CALC.EXE, CALENDAR.EXE, CARDFILE.EXE, CLOCK.EXE, and so on, which will start a familiar application when you double-click its name. Try it with the CLOCK.EXE, then look for another file within the WINDOWS directory with the name MSDOS.EXE. When you locate it double-click at its name. The program now running is the MS-DOS Executive which is a simpler and earlier version of File Manager. Try exploring the various commands of this program to see how many are similar to those of File Manager. By doing so you will learn a lot about both programs.

Next, change directory to the root directory, double click on the C:\ to reveal the files within the root directory and double-click the COMMAND.COM file. Windows will exit temporarily to DOS into its own window and you must type EXIT to return to the previous application. It has the same effect as double-clicking the the DOS Prompt icon of the 'Main' group. Try it.

Print Manager

You can use Print Manager to print information from a Windows application. Obviously, there might be some differences from one application to another, but these are slight.

When you print from a Windows application, the application creates a print file which is sent to the Windows Print Manager. From then on, Print Manager looks after the printing, queueing print files as they are sent to it, and freeing the application so that you can carry on working while files are being printed. It is assumed, of course, that you have installed your printer and configured it, using the Control Panel. If you have not, then double-click at the Control Panel icon of the 'Main' group of applications and then double-click at the Printers icon of the displayed Control Panel window, as explained in Chapter 1.

When you print from a non-Windows application that you have started from within Windows, the application does not use Print Manager - it prints just as it would if you had started it direct from the DOS Prompt.

The Print Queue:

When you print to a local printer, Print Manager maintains a local print queue which is a list of files that have been sent from an application to the printer. When Print Manager starts printing to a local queue, its icon appears at the bottom of your screen and enlarging it allows you to see the print queue, as follows:

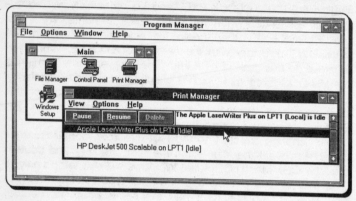

The above screen was obtained by double-clicking at the Notepad icon of the Accessories group of applications, then selecting the **File, Open** command, loading the **readme.txt** file, then using the **File, Print** command, double-clicking at the Print Manager icon, and pressing the **Pause** button. Printing can be resumed by pressing the **Resume** button.

You can even change the order of printing of files to a local printer by simply selecting the name of the file you want to move and dragging it to the require position in the queue.

When Print Manager prints to a network queue, the file is sent directly to the network print server. To see the state of the queue, you must double-click at the Print Manager icon of the Main group of applications - there is no Print Manager icon at the bottom of your screen as there was when printing locally. However, you cannot change the order of files in a network queue.

Finally, you can delete a file from a print queue, by selecting the file and pressing the **Delete** button on the Print Manager window, or you can delete all files in the queue by choosing the **Options, Exit** command, and pressing the **OK** button of the displayed confirmation dialogue box.

4. THE WINDOWS WRITE

Windows comes equipped with a reasonably powerful word processor called Write, which is found in the Accessories group of applications. It has all the normal editing features, including the ability to insert, delete, erase, search for, replace, copy and move characters, lines and whole blocks of text.

Write allows you to enhance text and create bold, underlined, italic, superscript, and subscript characters. You can even use different size fonts within the same document, and embed parts of graphics pictures which you might have created in another Windows application, using the Clipboard.

Word Processor Basics

To access the word processor double-click at the Write icon in the Accessories group of applications. A Windows screen similar to that shown below will appear, and a document named [Untitled] will open on your screen. When you save your work later you should give the document a meaningful name (no more than 8 characters in length) so that you can identify its contents easily from the actual name of the document.

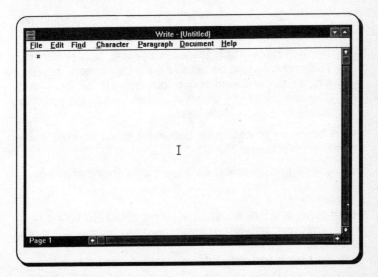

The Word Processor Screen:
The top line of the Write screen is the 'Title' bar which contains the name of the document, and if this bar is dragged with the mouse the window can be moved around the screen. Also, just like any other window, its size can be changed by dragging any of its four sides in the required direction.

The second line of the screen displays the 'Menu' bar which allows access to the following sub menus:

<u>F</u>ile <u>E</u>dit Fi<u>n</u>d <u>C</u>haracter <u>P</u>aragraph <u>D</u>ocument <u>H</u>elp

As described in Chapter 2 - 'Working with Windows' - the sub-menus are accessed either with your mouse, or by pressing the <Alt> key followed by the underlined letter.

If your system is set up for a mouse, the scroll bars, boxes and arrows described in Chapter 2, also appear on the right and bottom of the work area which makes up the remainder of the screen. To the left of the horizontal scroll bar at the bottom of the screen, there is a small area in which the page status is displayed.

Whenever a new Write file is opened two marks always appear in the top left corner of the working area of the screen. These are:

| the blinking vertical line is the cursor. Any text typed will be placed at this position.

¤ the end mark which identifies the end of a document. This mark cannot be erased from the screen. All text, etc., must be placed above this mark. It can be forced down the screen by pressing <Enter>, when the cursor is above it, to insert blank lines.

If you have paginated your document, then a third mark appears on the screen. This is:

» the page mark which identifies the beginning of a page.

Entering Text:
Before going any further, type the memo displayed on the next page. The text will be used to illustrate many of Write's capabilities.

As you type in text, any time you want to force a new line, or paragraph, just press <Enter>. While typing within a paragraph,

Write sorts out line lengths automatically, without you having to press any keys to move to a new line. This is known as 'word wrap'. If you make a mistake while typing, press the <BkSp> key enough times to erase the mistake and type the text again.

If you would like to type text at a position which is indented from the left margin (like the last entry of the text below), use the <Tab> key before typing the information. Write has tab stops at every half inch by default. How to exploit tabs to format your document, will be discussed at some length later on.

MEMO TO PC USERS

The microcomputers in the DP room are a mixture of IBM PS/2s (with 3.5" drives of 1.44MB capacity), IBM ATs (with 5.25" high density drives of 1.2MB capacity) and some IBM compatible machines, which are connected to various printers. As these only have 5.25" drives of 360kB capacity, before printing a document it must be saved on a 360kB format disc.

The computer you are using will have at least a 20MB hard disc on which a number of software programs have been installed. To make life easier, the hard disc is highly structured with each program installed in a separate directory. On switching the computer on, the following prompt is displayed:

C:\>

As you type into Write, sometimes you might notice large gaps at the end of lines, or between words if justification is switched on. You can eliminate such gaps by inserting an optional hyphen somewhere within the long word following the gap, by using the <Ctrl+Shift+Hyphen (-)> key stroke. Optional hyphens are invisible, unless they can appear at the end of a line.

Moving Around a Document:
You can move the cursor around a document with the normal direction keys, with the key combinations shown overleaf, or if you have paginated the document, with the **Find, Go To Page** command (or press **F4**), which allows you to jump to a specified page number. The 5, appearing in the list of key combinations listed overleaf, is the 5 on the keypad, while the 'direction' keys are listed by their function. Thus, RIGHT is used to indicate that you press the right-arrow key.

To move	Press
Left one character	LEFT
Right one character	RIGHT
Up one line	UP
Down one line	DOWN
Left one word	Ctrl+LEFT
Right one word	Ctrl+RIGHT
Beginning of line	HOME
End of line	END
Previous sentence	5+LEFT
Next sentence	5+RIGHT
Previous paragraph	5+UP
Next paragraph	5+DOWN
Up one window	PAGE UP
Down one window	PAGE DOWN
Top of window	Ctrl+PAGE UP
Bottom of window	Ctrl+PAGE DOWN
Previous page	5+PAGE UP
Next page	5+PAGE DOWN
To beginning of file	Ctrl+HOME
To end of file	Ctrl+END

Moving to the previous or next page of a document can only be achieved if you have paginated it first, using the **File, Repaginate** command.

Saving to a File:

To save a document, use the **File, Save As** command. A dialogue box appears on the screen, as shown below, with the

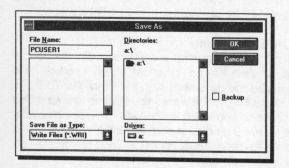

cursor in the 'File Name' field box waiting for you to type a name. You can select a drive other than the one displayed by clicking at the down arrow against the 'Drives' field. To save your work, move the cursor into the 'File Name' box, and type PCUSERS1. The program adds the extension WRI, automatically.

There are six formatting choices when you save a Write document. These are:

Use	*To Save As*
Write Files (.WRI)	A Write formatted document.
3.0 Write (.WRI)	A file that is compatible with Windows 3.0 - the option only appears if you have an embedded or linked object in the Write file.
Word for DOS (*.DOC)	A Microsoft Word document. Don't use this format if your document contains pictures. This format is not compatible with WinWord.
Word for DOS/Txt only	An unformatted Microsoft Word text file.
Text Files (*.TXT)	A Windows ANSI file. Use this option if your document is a program or you intend to telecommunicate it.
All Files (*.*)	An unformatted ASCII file.

Document Editing

It will not be long, when using Write, before you will need to edit your document. This could include deleting unwanted words, correcting a mistake or adding extra text in the document. All these operations are very easy to carry out.

For small deletions, such as letters or words, the easiest method to adopt is the use of the <Del> or <BkSp> keys. With the <Del> key, position the cursor on the first letter you want to delete and press <Del>; the letter is deleted and the following text moves one space to the left. With the <BkSp> key, position the cursor immediately to the right of the character to be deleted and press <BkSp>; the cursor moves one space to the left pulling the rest of the line with it and overwriting the character to be deleted. Note that the difference between the two is that with <Del> the cursor does not move at all.

Word processing is carried out in the insert mode. Any characters typed will be inserted at the cursor location and the following text will be pushed to the right, and down, to make room. To insert blank lines in your text, place the cursor at the beginning of the line where the blank is needed and press <Enter>. To remove the blank line position the cursor at its leftmost end and press <Del>.

When larger scale editing is needed, use the **Cut**, **Copy** and **Paste** operations, the text to be altered must be 'selected' before the operation can be carried out. These functions are then available when the **Edit** sub-menu is activated.

Selecting Text:
The procedure in Write, before any operation such as formatting or editing can be carried out on text, is first to select the text to be altered. Selected text is highlighted on the screen. This can be carried out in several ways:

a. Using the keyboard; position the cursor on the first character to be selected and hold down the <Shift> key while using the direction keys to highlight the required text, then release the <Shift> key. Navigational key combinations can be used with the <Shift> key to highlight blocks of text. For example, to highlight the text from the present cursor position to the end of the line, use <Shift+End>, while to highlight the text from the present cursor position to the end of the document, use <Shift+Ctrl+End>.

b. With the mouse; click the left mouse button at the beginning of the block and drag the cursor across the block so that the desired text is highlighted, then release the mouse button. To select a word, double-click at the word, to select a sentence, hold the <Ctrl> key down and click at the first word of the sentence, or to select a larger block, place the cursor at the beginning of the block, press the <Shift> key down and while holding it pressed, move the mouse pointer to the end of the desired block, and click the left mouse button.

c. Using the 'selection area' and a mouse; place the mouse pointer in the left margin area of the Write window where the mouse pointer changes to an arrow that slants to the right, and click the left mouse button once to select the current line, or twice to select the current paragraph.

Try out all these methods and find out the one you are most comfortable with.

Copying Blocks of Text:

Once text has been selected it can be copied to another location in your present document, to another Write document, or even to another Windows application. As with most of the editing and formatting operations there are two ways of doing this. The first is by using the **Edit, Copy** command sequence from the menu, moving the cursor to the start of where you want the copied text, and using the **Edit, Paste** command. The other method uses the quick key combination - <Ctrl+Ins> (or <Ctrl+C>) to copy and <Shift+Ins> (or <Ctrl+V>) to paste - once the text to be copied has been selected, which does not require the menu bar to be activated. As you get used to the Write package you will be able to save a lot of time by using quick key combinations.

To copy the same text again to another location in the document, move the cursor to the new location and paste it there with either method.

Moving Blocks of Text:

Selected text can be moved to any location in the same document. Use either the **Edit, Cut,** command or <Shift+Del> (or <Ctrl+X>), move the cursor to the required new location and use either the **Edit, Paste** command or <Shift+Ins> (or <Ctrl+V>). The moved text will be placed at the cursor location and will force any existing text to make room for it. This operation can be cancelled by simply pressing <Esc>.

Deleting Blocks of Text:

When text is deleted it is removed from the document. With Write any selected text can be deleted by pressing **Edit, Cut,** or by simply pressing the <Del> key. However, using **Edit, Cut,** allows you to use the **Edit, Paste** command, while using the <Del> key, does not.

The Undo Command:

As text is lost with the delete command you should use it with caution, but if you do make a mistake all is not lost as long as you act immediately. The **Edit, Undo Typing** command reverses your most recent editing or formatting command, so you need to use it before carrying out any further operations. The quick key for this command is <Alt+BkSp> (or <Ctrl+Z>).

Finding and Changing Text:

Write allows you to search for specifically selected text, or character combinations. In the 'Find' mode it will highlight each occurrence in turn so that you can carry out some action on it, such as change its font or appearance. In the 'Replace' mode you specify what replacement is to be automatically carried out.

For example, in a long article you may decide to replace every occurrence of the word 'programme' with the word 'program'. This is very easy to do. First go to the beginning of the file, as search only operates in a forward direction, then choose the **Find** command from Write's menu bar which reveals a pull-down sub-menu. You can then select either the **Find** or the **Replace** option. In the screen dump below, both dialogue boxes are shown in the same display for convenience.

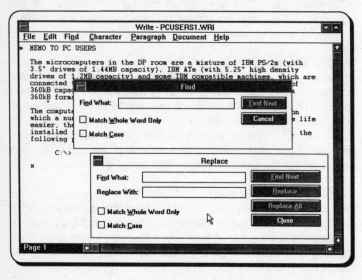

As can be seen, with both types of search you can type what you want to search for in the 'Find What' box. You can then specify whether you want to 'Match a Whole Word Only', and whether to 'Match a Case', by check-marking the appropriate boxes.

In the case of the 'Replace' dialogue box, you also have to type the replacement word in the 'Replace With' box, and then make an appropriate selection from the four buttons provided.

Selecting the **<Replace>** button requires you to manually confirm each replacement, whilst selecting the **<Replace All>** button will replace all occurrences of the word automatically. Write automatically matches the capitalisation of any text it replaces. If the replaced word is at the beginning of a sentence it will capitalise the first letter.

You can search for, and replace, special characters, or a combination of text and special characters (for example, tab or paragraph marks or white space). White space is a combination of any number of consecutive spaces and tab marks. A useful example of this is when you would like to find a specific word which occurs at the beginning of a paragraph, or after a tab.

The list below gives the key combinations of special characters to type into 'Find What' and 'Replace With' boxes.

Type	To find or replace
^w	A space anywhere in a document
^t	A tab character
^p	A paragraph mark
^d	A manual page break
?	Any character in a file. For example, searching for nec? will find such words as necessary, neck, nectar, and connect, to mention but a few, provided they exist in your document.

Page Breaks:

The program automatically inserts a page break in a document when a page of typed text is full and you have used the **File, Repaginate** command. The page break symbol (») tells the printer where to end one page and start printing another. If you select the 'Confirm Page Breaks' box in the Repaginate Document dialogue box, Write will ask for confirmation. When Write inserts a page break automatically, it prevents a single line in a paragraph from being printed by itself at the top or bottom of a page.

To force a manual page break in a document, use the key combination <Ctrl+Enter>. The resulting page break symbol in this case is a complete row of dots and Write readjusts all the non-manual page breaks for the remainder of the document. Manual page breaks can be selected, deleted, or copied.

Formatting Your Work

Formatting can involve the appearance of individual characters or words, the line spacing and alignment of paragraphs, and the overall page layout of the entire document. These functions are carried out with Write by selecting the **Character**, **Paragraph**, and/or **Document** commands from Write's menu bar.

Formatting Characters:

When you use Write for the first time, the fonts that you can use with it to format characters and words include Courier, Helvetica and AvantGarde, which are accessed with the **Character** command. Additional fonts depend on the printer(s) you have set-up and can be accessed from the **Character**, **Fonts** command, as shown below:

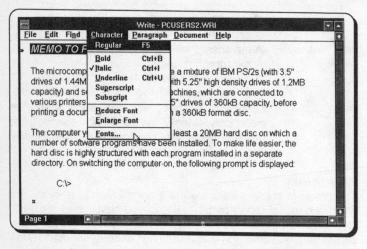

Originally, the text of the PC Users' memo was typed in Courier 10 point size. To change it into what appears on the above screen dump, first select the main body of the text, then use the **Fonts** option to format it in Helvetica 12 point size. The title of the memo was subsequently formatted in italics Helvetica 14 point size, as shown in the 'Font' dialogue box on the next page. If you can't access the aforesaid font styles, it would be because your printer does not support them. You can always choose one that your printer supports to see the difference. Save the result under the filename PCUSERS2.

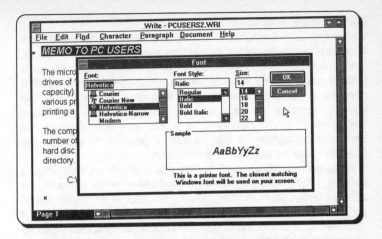

A 'point' is a unit of measurement, approximately 1/72 of an inch, that determines the height of a character. There is another unit of character measurement called the 'pitch' which is the number of characters that can fit horizontally in one inch. The spacing of a font is either 'fixed' (monospaced) or 'proportional'. With fixed spacing, each character takes up exactly the same space, while proportionally spaced characters take up different spacing (an 'i' or a 't' take up less space than a 'u' or a 'w'). Thus the length of proportionally spaced text can vary depending on which letters it contains. However, numerals take up the same amount of space whether they have been specified as fixed or proportional.

Which fonts you choose is largely dependent on your printer, as mentioned previously. One thing you must bear in mind is that Write uses screen fonts to display characters on screen and printer fonts to print characters with a printer. If you choose printer fonts for which there are no screen fonts, Write will use the nearest screen font to display your work, which might not be exactly what you will see when you print your work. It will be the printed document which is in the correct font style.

Windows 3.1 makes available several 'TrueType' fonts which can be used by Windows applications, such as Write. TrueType fonts are scalable to any point size and look exactly the same on the screen as they do when printed. These fonts appear in both Write's and Paintbrush's Font dialogue box with a TT symbol preceding them (see Courier New in above display).

Formatting Paragraphs:

Write defines a paragraph, as any text which is followed by a paragraph mark (which is created by pressing the <Enter> key, but is invisible unless selected, in which case it appears as a black square - once selected it can be deleted like any other character). So single line titles, as well as long typed text, can form paragraphs. All paragraph formatting, such as alignment, line spacing, and indentation, is stored in the marker for the particular paragraph. If this marker is deleted, or moved, the formatting will be deleted or moved with it.

Write allows you to align a paragraph at the left margin (the default), right margin, justified between both margins, or centred between both margins. A paragraph can be displayed on screen or paper in single-line spacing, 1½-line spacing, or double-line spacing. All alignment and spacing options can be selected from the **Paragraph** command.

Most documents with lists, or numbered sections, will require some form of paragraph indenting. An indent is the space between the margin and the edge of the text in the paragraph. This can be on the left or right side of the page. Open the file PCUSERS2, place the cursor in the first paragraph, and select the **Paragraph** command. The following pull-down menu will appear from which you can get the Indents dialogue box by choosing the **Indents** option.

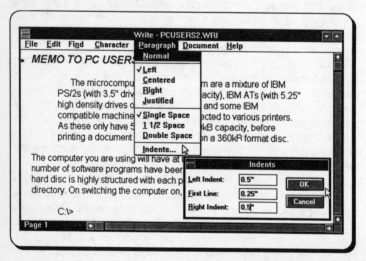

In the previous screen, both the **Character** sub-menu and the 'Indents' dialogue box are shown together for convenience. The first paragraph is shown indented which will be the result of typing the values shown in the 'Indents' dialogue box and pressing the **OK** button.

The **Indents** option can be used to create 'hanging' indents. To illustrate the method, use the PCUSERS1 file and add at the end of it, after the 'C:\>' prompt, the text shown below. After you have typed it in, save the resultant memo as PCUSERS3, before going on with formatting the new information. This is done as a precaution in case anything goes wrong with the formatting - it is much easier to reload a saved file (using the **File, Open** command), than it would be to try to unscramble a wrongly formatted document!

To find out what is on your hard disc, type

dir   (and press the <Enter> key)

which will produce a list of all the directories and filenames on the 'Root' directory (the one with the C:\> prompt) - directories are displayed with their names in angle brackets, for example, <DOS>. If your hard disc is structured correctly, then each program package will be installed in a separate directory. For example:

Name Description

LOTUS Holds the LOTUS 1-2-3 spreadsheet package.

QBASIC Holds the Quick Basic suite of programs which allow you to write fully structured Basic programs and compile them. It is one of the best version of Basic available.

QA Holds the Q&A package which is an integrated Database and Word Processor.

In general, using a computer effectively involves learning the operating system, in this case PC/MS-DOS, and then learning each package you are going to use.

Now select the text beginning with the line 'Name Description' and ending with the line 'Word Processor', then choose the **Paragraph, Indents** command, and type in the first two field boxes of the revealed 'Indents' dialogue box the values shown overleaf.

Note that the numbers you type in the first two fields of the dialogue box must be the same, but the first one, within the 'Left Indent' field, must be a positive number, while the second one, within the 'First Line' field, must be a negative number.

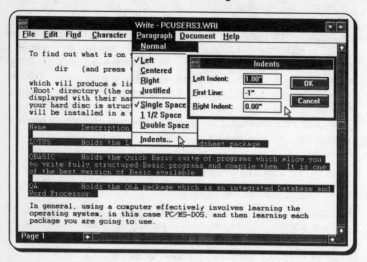

Pressing the **OK** button of the Indents dialogue box, produces the following display:

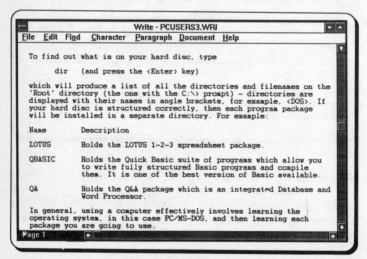

Indenting paragraphs is different from changing the left or right margins, as indents are counted 'from' the current margin settings. Therefore, if you were thinking of changing the page margins, you should do so first before indenting paragraphs.

When you are satisfied that all is as it should be, save the resultant formatted document under its current filename by simply using the **File, Save** command. This command does not display a dialogue box.

Formatting Documents:

The **Document** sub-menu holds all the commands which affect the layout of a document as a whole. From this sub-menu you can select options to display a ruler at the top of the text area of your screen so that you can set and see 'tabulation' points for your text, produce 'headers' which is text that appears at the top of every page, produce 'footers' which is text that appears at the bottom of every page, or change the 'margins' which is the space surrounding the text area of your document.

To illustrate the use of tabs, you will need to enter some more text which you should type into the PCUSERS3 document, starting after the end of the first paragraph. However, before starting to type, use the **Document, Ruler On** command to display a ruler along the top of your screen, as shown overleaf. The ruler shows the length of lines, the left and right margin positions and any tab and/or indent settings active in the paragraph the cursor is on.

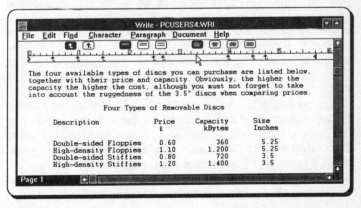

The ruler also displays three sets of icons which, if you have a mouse, can be used to change paragraph formats. The first set of ruler icons contains two tab icons (for normal and decimal tabulation). The second set contains three line spacing icons (for single-line spacing, 1½-line spacing, and double-line spacing), while the third set contains four alignment icons for aligning text at the left or right margin, centring it between both margins, or justifying it between both margins. To use these formatting capabilities, simply place the cursor in the paragraph you would like to format and then click at the appropriate icon.

Setting your own tabs is easy by either typing in the distances for the tab points (in inches) in the Tabs dialogue box which can be selected from the **Document** sub-menu, or by using the mouse to click at either the left-aligned tab icon (the one with the curly tail) or the decimal tab icon (the one with the straight tail and dot next to it) and then click within the ruler where you want to set the tab. Tabs can be moved within the ruler by dragging them with the mouse to a new position or even remove them by simply dragging them off the ruler.

Default tab settings do not show on the ruler, but custom tabs do. All default tabs to the left of a new custom tab are removed automatically, so make sure you insert as many as you need to format the whole of your document. You can set up to 12 tabs - either left-aligned tabs or decimal tabs. Decimal tabs allow you to align numbers on their decimal point, thus allowing the formation of neat columns. If you type text at a decimal tab, the characters you type are inserted to the left of the tab until you type a period. This effect can be used to right-align text.

Now insert into the ruler all the tabs shown above and type the text shown, aligning the various parts of it to the appropriate tab points by pressing the <Tab> key prior to typing the relevant information. When you finish, save the resultant work as PCUSERS4.

In a printed document a 'header' is text that appears at the top of each page of the document, whilst a 'footer' appears at the bottom, which can be used to add titles and page numbers. Depending on where you want your page numbers to appear, choose **Header** or **Footer** from the **Document** sub-menu which will reveal an appropriate dialogue box on an empty header or footer document window, as shown on the next page.

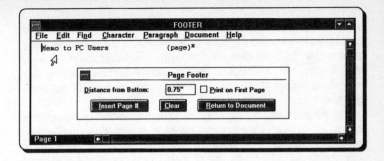

It is in this window you type the header or footer text (in the above screen this appears as 'Memo to PC Users'), then press the **Insert Page #** button in the dialogue box which causes the bracketed word '(page)' to appear at the end of the header or footer text. Both the header or footer text, and the word '(page)', can be formatted from the **Paragraph** sub-menu (this was done for '(page)' only in the above example).

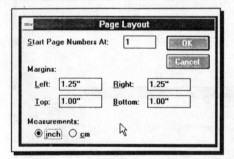

The actual starting page number of your document can be set by selecting the **Page Layout** option from the **Document** sub-menu which displays the 'Page Layout' dialogue box, as shown opposite.

It is also in this dialogue box that you can change the page margins from their displayed default values. Of course, the actual page layout is dependent on the installed printer and its set-up (size of paper selected and orientation), as discussed next.

Printing Documents

When Windows was first installed on your computer the printers you intend to use should have been selected, which would have caused the SETUP program to copy the appropriate printer drivers from the distribution discs. Before printing for the first time, it is essential to ensure that your printer is properly installed.

Best output results can only be obtained when using a laser printer. So, if you want to produce high-quality documents, and you have access to a laser printer (even if not connected to your computer), then use the procedure on 'Installing a Printer', discussed in Chapter 1, to install the laser printer as an additional printer to be used with Windows and configure it to print to 'File'. Next, activate Write and use the **File, Print Setup** command and highlight the chosen printer in the 'Print Setup' dialogue box, as shown below:

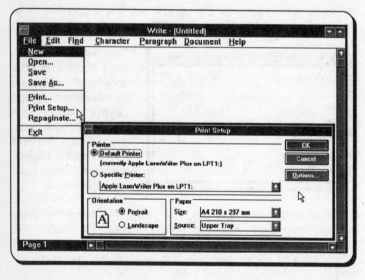

From the 'Print Setup' dialogue box you can select the default printer or any of the other printers you have installed during installation. Again, this dialogue box is shown on the same screen dump as the **File** sub-menu for convenience. It is in this last dialogue box that you set the paper size and its orientation.

From then on, you can use the **File, Print** command from within Write to send print output to either the printer connected to your computer or to an encoded file on disc. Such a file can be printed on a laser printer by using the DOS command

COPY *Filename*/B LPT1

on the computer connected to it, without needing to install Windows on it.

Do remember that, whenever you change printers, the appearance of your document might change as Write uses the fonts available with the newly selected printer. This can affect the line lengths, which in turn will affect tabulation, and page breaks. To see the new page breaks, use the **File, Repaginate** command, as explained earlier.

Including Pictures in Write
There are three ways in which you can include a picture within `Write document; copy, embed or link.

Copying a Picture into Write:
You might have noticed that in Write's **Edit** sub-menu there are two options available which allow you to move and size pictures. This is because you can cut and paste graphics pictures from other Windows applications, in the same way as you can with text, using the Windows' Clipboard accessory.

Write's ability to include pictures in a document is illustrated below with a step-by-step example which, however, requires you to use the Paintbrush module - the use of which has not, as yet, been discussed. Nevertheless, if you follow the suggested steps, you will not find any difficulty in using it at this stage.

What we are after is to paste Write's icon on the latest version of the memo to PCUSERS. To do so, we will copy the icons of Write and Paintbrush to a new applications group, capture the window of this group on the Clipboard, use the Paintbrush module to extract the desired icon, and paste it on our memo. The required steps to do this are as follows:

- Select the Program Manager's **File, New** command which displays the 'New Program Object' dialogue box,

- Click at the Program Group option and press the **OK** button which causes the display of the 'Program Properties' dialogue box,

- Enter the name 'WP' in the Description field and press the **OK** button which causes the WP group window to be displayed,

- Size the WP group window to approximately 1" x 1" and press the **Ctrl** key and while keeping it pressed, drag the Write application icon to a position within the WP window. Release the mouse button and the **Ctrl** key to fix the copy of Write's icon in WP,

- Repeat the last step above, but this time copy the Paintbrush icon into the WP window,

- Close all application windows, except the WP window which you should then move close to the top-left corner of the Program Manager's working area,

- Press the <Print Screen> key on your keyboard which has the effect of copying everything on your screen to the Clipboard,

- Double-click on the Paintbrush icon and select the **Edit, Paste** command from Paintbrush's menu bar to paste the contents of the Clipboard into Paintbrush's working area, then click on the top-right icon of the Tool Bar which Paintbrush displays on the left side of your screen (the one with the image of scissors cutting a square shape). Next, move the mouse pointer (it now has the shape of a cross) to a position just above and to the left of the Write icon, press the left mouse button and drag the mouse to a position just to the right and below the Write icon. As you are dragging the mouse a dotted oblong is formed, the aim being to surround the icon. Releasing the mouse button fixes the dotted oblong around the icon which is the shape we would like to save. If you make a mistake, click at the right scissors icon of the Tool Bar and repeat the steps required to mark the cut-out,

- Use the **Edit, Cut** command from within Paintbrush which automatically places the cut-out on the Clipboard, and close the Paintbrush application,

- Double-click on the Write icon and select the **File, Open** command to load the latest version of your memo to PCUSERS,

- Use the **Edit, Paste** command which pastes a copy of the Write icon from the Clipboard onto the memo at a position near the left margin on the line the cursor is on,

- Click at the image of the picture to highlight it, then use the **Edit, Move Picture** command to move it horizontally to the desired position,

- Use the **Edit, Size Picture** command to size the picture to your requirement.

When you paste a graphics picture into Write, it always appears at the left margin. Hence, you are given the option to select it and move it horizontally, as well as change its size. Do remember, however, that Write displays pictures in screen resolution appropriate to the printer you have selected, and as a result of differences in printer resolution, pictures might appear distorted on screen. However, when you print a Write document which incorporates a picture, its resolution will be correct.

The following few lines of the PCUSERS memo was printed on a PostScript printer.

MEMO TO PC USERS

The microcomputers in the DP room are a mixture of IBM PS/2s (with 3.5" drives of 1.44MB capacity), IBM ATs (with 5.25" high density drives of 1.2MB capacity) and some IBM compatible machines, which are connected to various printers. As these only have 5.25" drives of 360kB capacity, before printing a document it must be saved on a 360kB format disc.

The four available types of discs you can purchase are listed below, together with their price and capacity. Obviously, the higher the capacity the higher the cost, although you must not forget to take into account the ruggedness of the 3.5" discs when comparing prices.

Embedding a Picture into Write:
Embedding a picture or a drawing into Write is similar to copying, but with one important advantage: You can actually edit an embedded object, because you can open Paintbrush from within Write.

Obviously, you can only use other applications in place of Write and Paintbrush to embed pictures or drawings, if these applications are capable of supporting embedding.

To embed a Paintbrush drawing into Write, transfer the drawing from Paintbrush onto the Clipboard, as detailed previously under 'Copying a Picture into Write', then use the **Edit, Paste** command from within Write.

Linking a Picture into Write:
The advantage of linking files dynamically is that it allows information held in one file to be automatically updated when the information in the other file changes.

To link a Paintbrush drawing into Write, transfer it from Paintbrush to the Clipboard, then use the **Edit, Paste Special** command from within Write.

5. THE WINDOWS PAINTBRUSH

You can use the Paintbrush module to create simple or complicated colour pictures. Obviously, the use of the mouse is almost mandatory, if you are about to express yourself with sweeping movements. Nevertheless, you can still use the keyboard to create some drawings, but it is rather cumbersome. For this reason the instructions given in this section are almost exclusively directed to mouse users, but the equivalent keystrokes are listed below.

Mouse Action	Equivalent Keystrokes
Click the left button	Press the <Ins> key
Click the right button	Press the <Del> key
Double-click the left button	Press the F9+<Ins> keys
Double-click the right button	Press the F9+<Del> keys
Drag the cursor	Press <Ins>+Arrow key.

As you can see, unlike the other Windows programs, Paintbrush makes use of both the left and the right mouse buttons. When you are asked to click the mouse button, without specifying which one, then use the left mouse button. If you need to click or double-click the right mouse button, it will be specified.

Starting Paintbrush

To start Paintbrush, double-click at the Paintbrush icon (the stylized artist's palette and brush) which is to be found in the Accessories group of programs. A few seconds later, the 'Untitled' Paintbrush opening screen will be displayed, as shown overleaf.

The screen is divided into a 'drawing' area (the default size of which depends on your video display), surrounded by the 'menu bar' at the top, the 'Palette' at the bottom, the 'Line-size' box at the bottom-left corner, and the 'Toolbox' at the left. The drawing area is where you create your paintbrush drawings with the help of various tools from the 'Toolbox', whose names are listed within the drawing area in the screen dump overleaf with the first name in each box referring to the leftmost tool. Exactly what functions these tools allow you to perform, are also listed below the screen dump.

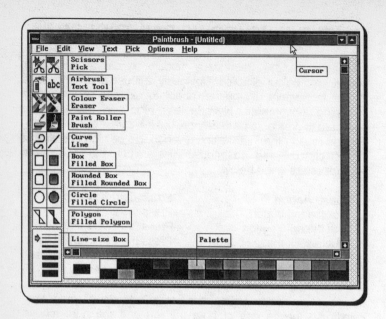

Note that the 'brush' tool is always selected when you start Paintbrush. To select any other tool, simply point to it and click. Their function is listed below.

Tool	*Function*
Scissors	Used to cutout an irregular-shaped area of a picture which can then be dragged to another part of the drawing, or manipulated using the **Edit** menu commands,
Pick	Used to cut out a rectangular-shaped area of a picture which can then be dragged to another part of the drawing, or manipulated using the **Edit** menu commands,
Airbrush	Used to produce a circular spray in the current foreground colour,

Text Tool	Used to add text of several different fonts and type sizes, to drawings, in the current foreground colour,
Colour Eraser	Used to change the selected foreground colours under the eraser icon to a background colour, or automatically change every occurrence of one colour in the drawing area to another,
Eraser	Used to change any colours under the eraser icon into the current background colour,
Paint Roller	Used to fill in any closed shape or area with the current foreground colour,
Brush	Used to add freehand shapes and lines in the current foreground colour and drawing width,
Curve	Used to generate curved lines in the current foreground colour and drawing width,
Line	Used to generate straight lines between two points in the current foreground colour and drawing width,
Box	Used to draw hollow squares or rectangles in the current foreground colour and drawing width,
Filled Box	Used to draw filled squares or rectangles in the current foreground colour,
Rounded Box	Used to draw hollow squares or rectangles with rounded corners in the current foreground colour and drawing width,

Filled Rounded Box	Used to draw filled squares or rectangles with rounded corners in the current foreground colour,
Circle	Used to draw hollow circles or ellipses in the current foreground colour and drawing width,
Filled Circle	Used to draw filled circles or ellipses in the current foreground colour,
Polygon	Used to draw hollow triangles and other multi-sided irregular shapes in the current foreground colour and drawing width,
Filled Polygon	Used to draw filled triangles and other multi-sided irregular shapes in the current foreground colour.

Preparing for a Drawing

Before you start drawing, you might decide to change the thickness of lines, from their default value, that you use with the various drawing tools, and/or change the foreground and background colours of your drawing from the default colours which are white for background and black for foreground, as shown at the bottom of your screen, and identified below:

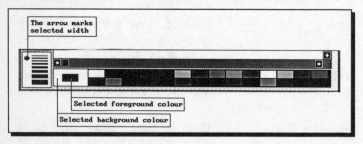

Selecting the Drawing Width:

To change the drawing widths of lines or borders around boxes from their default value, point to the width you want to use in the Line-size box and click the left mouse button. The arrow that marks the current width, will move to point to the selected width.

Selecting the Background Colour:

To select a new background colour, point to the colour (or pattern, if you have configured your system as monochrome) in the Palette and click the right mouse button. If you now select the **File**, **New** command, Paintbrush will open a new document with the selected background colour or pattern in the drawing area. Only by choosing the **File**, **New** command, can you change the background colour for the entire drawing area.

The background colour used, can be changed at any time during a drawing session to create special effects with tools and commands that use the background colour to draw, such as shadows around objects.

Selecting the Foreground Colour:

To select a different foreground colour to be used with any of the drawing tools in the Toolbox, point to the colour or pattern in the Palette and click the left mouse button.

Entering Text in a Drawing:

If you intend to enter text within a drawing, carry out the following steps:

- Select the foreground colour for the text
- Select the **Text** tool from the Toolbox
- Select the character font you want to use
- Select the point size for the font
- Select the style for the font
- Select the position of the text and type it.

If you unsure of what is meant by font, point size or font style, refer to the section entitled 'Formatting Characters' in the previous chapter.

To select a font, use the **Text**, **Fonts** command from Paintbrush's menu as shown overleaf. This causes a pull-down sub-menu of available fonts to be displayed, the number and type of font options being dependant on your particular printer. Selecting the name of a specific font from the **Font** field, causes the available point sizes for that font to be displayed in the **Size** field of the 'Font' dialogue box.

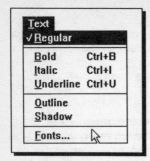

Once you have chosen the font and the point size you want to use for your text, you can either select the style of the characters from the Font Style field of the 'Font' dialogue box displayed below, or by selecting one or more of the options available in the **Text** sub-menu of Paintbrush, shown opposite, which include bold, italic, underline, outline, or shadow.

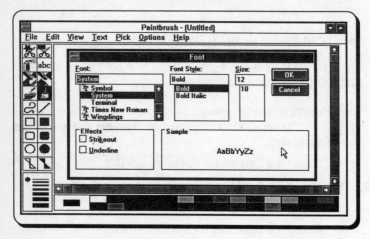

Using the Paintbrush Tools

Most of the tools in Paintbrush's Toolbox are quite easy and straightforward to use. To select a tool, point to it and click the left mouse button which causes its icon in the Toolbox to be highlighted. To use them, you are required to move the cursor to a suitable position within the drawing area and press the left mouse button and, while holding the mouse button depressed, move the tool around to accomplish the required task. Releasing the mouse button stops the action being performed.

In this way you can use most of Paintbrush's Toolbox tools. If you make any mistakes, how you correct these depends on the tool being used at the time. For example:

With the two 'Cutout' and two 'Polygon' tools, if you change your mind after you have released the mouse button, press the right mouse button to start again,

With the two 'Line', four 'Box', and two 'Circle' tools, if you change your mind before you release the mouse button, press the right mouse button to start again,

With the 'Airbrush', 'Paint Roller' and 'Brush' tools, if you change your mind and don't like what you are doing, you must use the two 'Eraser' tools.

Alternatively, you can eliminate everything you have been doing with a particular drawing tool by selecting the **Edit, Undo** command from the menu bar.

To complete this discussion, we need to describe how you should use the 'Curve', and 'Polygon' tools, which differ slightly from the rest. For example:

To draw a curve, place the cursor in the required starting position within the drawing area, then press the left mouse button to anchor the beginning of the curve and, while holding down the mouse button, move the mouse to the required end of the eventual curve and release it. A flexible line stretches between the two points. Next, press the left mouse button and drag the cursor in a direction away from the line, which causes the line to curve in that direction. When you are happy with the produced curvature, release the mouse button. If you want to curve the line in one direction only, click the end point of the curve once more; if you want to produce an 'S' curve, press the mouse button and drag the curve in the required second direction. On releasing the mouse button, the curved line is fixed in position and is coloured in the foreground colour.

To draw a polygon, place the cursor in the required starting point within the drawing area and press the mouse button, move the mouse to the required end of the first side of the polygon and release it. A flexible line stretches between the two points. Next, continue adding sides to the polygon until you complete the polygon, at which point you should double-click the mouse button.

When you are drawing a Filled Polygon, the selected drawing width determines the thickness of the polygon's border. If you don't want a border, make the foreground and background colours the same.

The best way of learning how to use the various drawing tools is to experiment. Do try drawing something of your choice and practising with all the available tools, before going on.

Advanced Paintbrush Features

In order to illustrate as many advanced Paintbrush functions as possible, we will devise an example that does not require you to be an artist before you can start. Instead, we will use an existing drawing that comes with the Paintbrush module to discuss these techniques.

To start with, clear you drawing screen of anything you might have on it, by selecting the **File, New** command from Paintbrush's menu bar. Then, select the **File, Open** command which causes the following 'Open' dialogue box to appear on your screen:

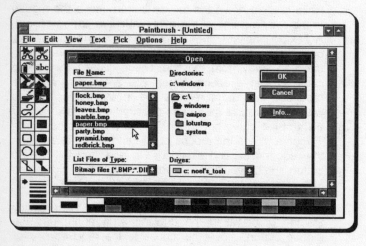

From the displayed files with the .bmp extension, select the **paper.bmp** file, which when loaded should appear on your screen as follows:

We will first select the Pick tool (the scissors with the oblong cut-out) to mark an oblong which surrounds the actual word 'Windows' from the present drawing, then use the **Edit, Copy** command to make a copy of the cut-out onto the Clipboard.

Next, choose the **File, New** command to clear the screen and then select the **Edit, Paste** command to paste the cut-out on your screen. The cut-out will be placed automatically at the top-left corner of your drawing area with the dotted line still around it. This means that you can move it to any other part of the screen by simply dragging it to a new location. Do just that, and move the cut-out to the top-right corner of your drawing area.

Note that when you mark a cut-out, the menu option **Pick** becomes available to you. If a cut-out is not marked, this option of the menu is dimmed. Clicking at this menu option reveals a sub-menu which is different to what you have been used to so far. It is from this sub-menu, shown below, that most of the advanced features of Paintbrush can be reached.

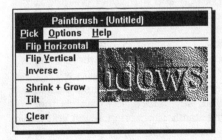

However, before you try any of these options, first save the cut-out, using the **File, Save As** command, under the filename **window1**, then adorn it with two borders (using the Box tool), the inner one with the thinnest line (selected from the Line-size box), and the outer with the fourth thickest line, as shown overleaf.

73

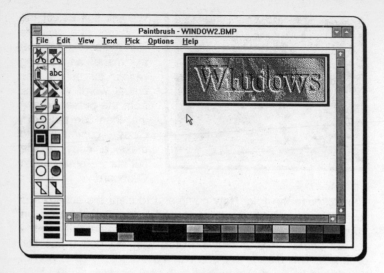

Having done so, use the **File, Save As** command and save it to disc under the filename **window2**, before going on to experiment with the **Pick** menu option. In this way you will have the **window1.bmp** and **window2.bmp** files safely on disc, ready to load them whenever you need them.

Tilting a Cut-out:

To illustrate how to tilt a cut-out, select the Pick tool (the scissors with the oblong cut-out) and mark your drawing close to the outer border. The dotted line of the cut-out should now make your drawing take the appearance of a serrated postage stamp. Next, select the **Pick, Tilt** command, place the cursor at the bottom-left corner of the drawing and press the left mouse button. A dotted outline of the shape of the drawing will appear on the screen with its top side anchored at the cursor position.

As you drag the mouse in, say, a direction towards the left, this dotted shape tilts in the same direction in which you move the mouse. Releasing the mouse button fixes the shape in the chosen tilted position and draws the picture appropriately tilted. If you now place the cursor at the bottom-left corner of this tilted shape and press the mouse button, then release it without moving the mouse, you will get a staircase effect, as shown on the next page.

74

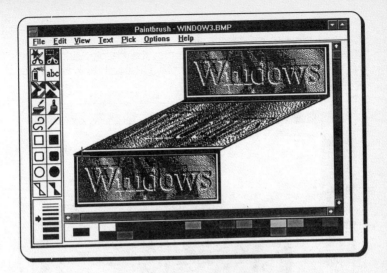

If you make a mistake and you want to start again from the beginning, use the **File, New** command to clear the screen, then the **File, Open** command to reload the **window2.bmp** file. If, on the other hand, you want to re-position your drawing after you have selected the **Pick, Tilt** command, then click once more at the Pick Tool (the scissors with the oblong cut-out) and use the mouse to mark the portion of the drawing you want to move.

Enlarging a Cut-out:

To illustrate cut-out enlargement, load the **window1.bmp** file, select the Pick tool and use the mouse to mark the edge of the picture.

Next, select the **Pick, Shrink & Grow** command and also click at the **Clear** option of the **Pick** sub-menu. This last option, when selected, clears the screen of the original drawing after it has been enlarged, shrunk, or tilted. If the **Clear** option is not selected (you know that it has because a check-mark appears against its name), the original cut-out remains on the screen. Now use the mouse to mark a square with a side of just over one-half of the length of the original cut-out. Save the resultant shape under the filename **window4**.

Finally, click at the Pick tool and use the mouse to mark the enlarged square, select the **Pick** command and click at the **Clear** option of the sub-menu so that the check-mark against the option is cleared, then select the **Tilt** command and try to produce the following drawing:

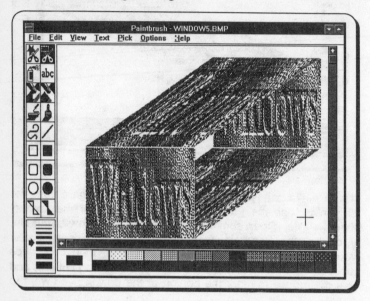

Copying a Cutout:
It is possible to move a cut-out and leave a copy of it at its original position. In addition, you can choose to paste the cut-out opaquely or transparently in its new location.

Thus, to move a cut-out and leave a copy behind, mark the part of the drawing you want to replicate, move the cursor within the cut-out, press the right mouse button to paste opaquely, or the left mouse button to paste transparently, then press the <Shift> key and while keeping it pressed down, drag the cut-out to its new position. Once the cut-out is where you would like it to be, release the <Shift> key first, then the mouse button.

* * *

There is no limit to what you can do with Paintbrush. All you need is imagination, a lot of patience and some artistic ability!

6. THE WINDOWS CARDFILE

A Windows Cardfile database is a file which contains related information, such as 'Company names', 'Addresses', 'Phone numbers', 'Contacts', etc. A phone book is a simple database stored on paper. In the case of Cardfile, to make the entry and access of data easier, the program emulates the traditional 5" x 7" index cards, with each card having an 'index field' - the first line on the card - which holds some unique information, such as the name of a company, that Cardfile uses to scan a database quickly in order to find a specific record.

Database Basics

The following section deals with the basic concepts of using a database, along with the database 'jargon' that is used in this book. If you are not familiar with database terminology then you should read this section first.

A database is a collection of data that exists, and is organised around a specific theme or requirement. A database is used for storing information (data) so that it is quickly accessible; data is stored in specially structured files that reside on disc like other disc-files.

We define a Cardfile database and its various elements as follows:

Database	A collection of data organised for a specific theme,
Data-file	Disc-file in which data is stored
Record	A Cardfile card on which information relating to a single entry is held
Index Field	A single line of information of the same type, such as names of companies
List	A screen-view mode in which records are displayed by their index field.

A good example of a database is a telephone list and, as you will know, to cover all your requirements, you might need many such lists. In the same way, a database can contain a number of data-files.

The following example shows how information is presented in a list of companies.

Erobase Co. Ltd., 33 Trevithick Road Truro 237186
Avon Construction, 15 Woodburn Road Bristol 678543
Barrows Associates, 42 North Gate Road Bodmin 395642
Stoneage Ltd., 38 Western Approach Plymouth 135791
Time & Motion, 4 Ruskin Crescent Maidenhead 664422
Parkway Gravel Ltd., 11 Woodland Avenue Exeter 891256
Vortex Co. Ltd., 91 Cabot Close London 546132
Westwood Ltd., 5 Benson Stree Brighton 986532
Hire Services, 123 North Circular Road London 214376

Information is structured in fields which are identified below, for a single record, as follows:

Company	Address	Town	Tel No
Eurobase Co. Ltd	33 Trevithick Road	Truro	237186

Unlike other databases, Cardfile has essentially only two fields; the 'Index' field, which in the above example is the 'Company', and the another field which contains the rest of the information. It does, however, recognise telephone numbers - more about this, later.

Creating a Cardfile Database

The following section deals with aspects relating to the design of a database. This includes considerations on entering, editing, and deleting data. In order to fully acquaint yourself with the Cardfile database, you are urged to enter in your own computer the examples discussed below. All the commands used can be and are executed from the menu system, although there are 'quick keys' available for nearly every option offered by Cardfile. These will be discussed later.

To create a Cardfile database, first start the Cardfile module, which is to be found in the Accessories group of applications, by double-clicking at its icon. Just as in the case of Write, when used for the first time, Cardfile creates an 'untitled' file as shown on the next page.

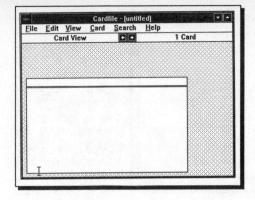

To add records to Cardfile, select the **Card, Add** command from the Cardfile menu (or simply press **F7**). The Add dialogue box appears on your screen with the cursor placed at the beginning of the **Add** field. Any information entered in this field (say, AAA) will appear in Cardfile's *index field*, the first line of a record, as shown below:

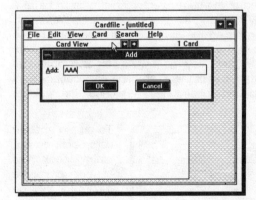

Pressing <Enter> transfers the information typed in (in this case, AAA) into the index field of a second card (an empty card appears behind it) with the cursor placed at the beginning of the main body of the card. It is at this point where you enter information, such as address, phone number, contact person, etc. However, since we are going to create several cards with the same basic information on each (we will design a skeleton card first), use the **Card, Delete** command to delete the first of the two cards (the one with the AAA entry). This is the way you can also delete unwanted cards at a later stage.

Next, type in the headings of the fields (Address, Phone, etc., in what will become our prototype card, the first card offered to you by Cardfile, as shown overleaf.

79

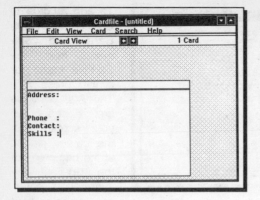

To add cards all we need to do is duplicate this card and edit it. To do so, select the **Card, Duplicate** command, followed by **Edit, Index** (or **F6**). This displays the Index dialogue box, allowing you to enter the index line (type Parkway Gravel Ltd and press <Enter>).

To edit the rest of the card, press the <End> key to relocate the cursor at the end of the current entry which should be at a position immediately following the first colon (**:**) after 'Address', where you can start typing the first line of the address of the relevant company. At the end of the line, press the <Down> arrow key (not the <Enter> key, as it will insert an empty line) followed by appropriate use of the <Tab> and <Spacebar> keys to align the second and subsequent lines under the first, as shown below:

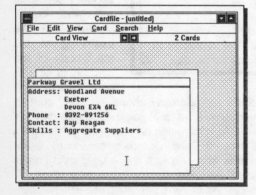

To create another card, click on the empty index field of our prototype record (or click on one of the two horizontal arrow-buttons displayed below Cardfile's menu bar, which allows you to browse through records) to display it on the front of the pack. Next, duplicate it and edit it (use the **Card, Duplicate** command, followed by **F6**). In this way, you don't have to retype the labels appearing to the left of the colons of each record.

Below are listed ten records, two of which you have already inserted in your database. Complete the rest of the entries, enter them in the order from left to right so that you deliberately avoid entering in alphabetical order.

Address:
 	
Phone :
Contact:
Skills :
	Parkway Gravel Ltd
	Address: 11 Woodland Avenue
	        Exeter
	        Devon EX4 6KL
	Phone : 0392-891256
	Contact: Ray Reagan
	Skills : Aggregate Suppliers

Avon Construction
Address: 15 Woodburn Road
        Bristol
        Avon BS11 2XE
Phone : 0272-678543
Contact: Tim Pruce
Skills : Adhesive Suppliers
	Stoneage Ltd
	Address: 38 Western Approach
	        Plymouth
	        Devon PL11 0QA
	Phone : 0752-135791
	Contact: Alex Pryor
	Skills : Carbon Dating

Barrows Associates
Address: 42 North Gate Road
        Bodmin
        Cornwall PL12 31XW
Phone : 0208-395642
Contact: Clive Price
Skills : Tunnel Design
	Time & Motion
	Address: 4 Ruskin Crescent
	        Maidenhead
	        Berks BE1 1EB
	Phone : 0628-664422
	Contact: Steve King
	Skills : Systems Analyst

Eurobase Co. Ltd
Address: 33 Trevithick Road
        Truro
        Cornwall TR2 5YU
Phone : 0872-237186
Contact: Mike Prowse
Skills : Project Management
	Vortex Co. Ltd
	Address: 4 Ruskin Crescent
	        Maidenhead
	        Berks BE1 1EB
	Phone : 0628-664422
	Contact: Steve King
	Skills : Systems Analyst

Hire Services
Address: Dolphin House
        123 North Circular Road
        London NW2 2TR
Phone : 081-214376
Contact: Kim Ford
Skills : Accountants
	Westwood Ltd
	Address: 5 Besnson Street
	        Fishergate
	        East Sussex BN5 9PL
	Phone : 0273-986532
	Contact: Helen Queen
	Skills : Seminar Organisers

Once you have finished entering all the records, use the **File**, **Save As** command and type CONTACTS. The program will add the filename extension .CRD automatically. If you try to exit Cardfile without saving, you will be prompted to remind you that you have not saved the changes made to your database.

Modes of Viewing Cardfile:

Cardfile records can be viewed in two modes. The first is the default mode, the one used to display your additions to the database so far, called the 'Card' mode which simulates cards in a box, as shown below:

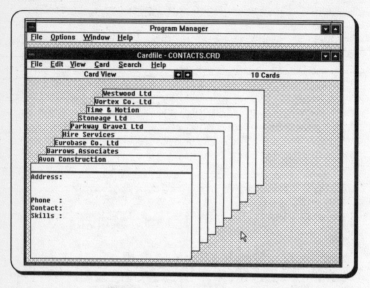

The second viewing mode is the 'List' mode obtained by selecting the **V̲iew, L̲ist** command. The result is shown below:

Note: Once you have either switched viewing modes, or saved and later reloaded your database, Cardfile displays automatically all records in alphabetical order. The front-most record in the Card mode is the *current* record which you have been editing or viewing. On switching the viewing mode to List, this record remains the current record and is shown highlighted.

Searching a Cardfile Database

You can search a Cardfile database either by its index field or by an item in the card.

To search by the index field, use the **Search, Go To** command (or press **F4**) and type any of the words in the index field in the displayed dialogue box. For example, press **F4** and type the word 'services'. Almost immediately the record 'Hire Services' is made the current record and appears at the forefront of the database cards.

To search by an item anywhere else on a card, use the **Search, Find** command and type the item you want to search the database with. For example, typing the name 'Reagan' finds the 'Parkway Gravel Ltd' record, and pressing **F3** finds the next record with the same item (in this case 'Vortex Co. Ltd')

Finally, if you would like to browse through records, then use the two horizontal arrow buttons on the status line.

Cardfile Keystrokes

When working with Cardfile you tend to use the keyboard far more than the mouse. Below we list several keystrokes which can be used to quickly accomplish certain results. These are:

Keystroke	Result
F3	Activate the Find dialogue box and find the next occurrence of an item
F4	Activate the Go To dialogue box to initiate an indexed search
F5	Activate the Autodial dialogue box for the current record
F6	Activate the Index dialogue box to edit the index field of the current record
F7	Activate the Add record dialogue box to add a record to the database
Ctrl+Home	Highlights the first record of the database and brings it to the forefront of the display
Ctrl+End	Highlights the last record of the database and brings it to the forefront of the display
PgDn	In card mode it scrolls forward one record at a time; in list mode it moves forward one window (page) at a time

PgUp	In card mode it scrolls backward one record at a time; in list mode it moves backward one window (page) at a time
Down arrow	In list mode it moves forward one record through the list of records
Up arrow	In list mode it moves backward one record through the list of records
Shift+Del	(Ctrl+X) has the same effect as Edit, Cut
Shift+Ins	(Ctrl+V) has the same effect as Edit, Paste
Ctrl+Ins	(Ctrl+C) has the same effect as Edit, Copy
Alt+BkSp	(Ctrl+Z) has the same effect as the Edit, Undo

The Cardfile Autodial Feature

If you have a modem, you can arrange for Cardfile to autodial a telephone number for you. Let us suppose you would like to dial Helen Queen. To get Cardfile to do it for you, simply select the **Search, Find** command and type 'Helen' in the displayed Find dialogue box. This will search the database and make the Westwood Ltd record the current record with the name Helen highlighted. Next, press one of the arrow keys to remove the highlighting and then select the **Card, Autodial** command (or press **F5**), which causes the top half of the following dialogue box to be displayed:

Pressing the Set-up button, reveals an additional part of the dialogue box which allows you to set the 'Dial Type' of your phone, the 'Baud Rate' of your modem, and the communications 'Port' you have connected it to. Normally you would have configured Windows to recognise and use your modem automatically, in which case you will not need to use the Setup button.

Pasting a Picture on a Card

There are three ways in which you can paste a picture on a card; copy, embed or link.

Copying and Pasting a Picture on a Card:

To paste a picture on a card, first copy the picture onto the Clipboard, by using the **Edit, Copy** command. This assumes that you have a picture of suitable size. However, let us assume that you would like to use something which appears on your screen when working in Windows, say, the Cardfile icon. To illustrate the process, arrange for the Program Manager to display the Accessories icons, and move the whole group of applications to a position close to the top-left corner of the screen, then

- Press the <Print Screen> key on your keyboard. This has the effect of capturing the whole screen on the Clipboard. You can check this by activating the Clipboard; if you do, exit from the Clipboard before going to the next step,

- Activate the Paintbrush module and select the **Edit, Paste** command, select the rectangular scissors from the Tools bar and mark a rectangle to surround the Cardfile icon. Then select the **Edit, Cut** command which transfers the marked cut-out to the Clipboard, and exit Paintbrush,

- Activate Cardfile and select the **File, Open** command and load your database, but before doing so, make sure you have a backup (see 'Warning', below),

- Make the card to which you want to transfer the picture the active record, and select the **Edit, Picture** command, followed by the **Edit, Paste** command which causes the picture to appear at the upper-left corner of the card,

- Drag the picture with the mouse or use the arrow keys to place it exactly where you want it on the card, and select the **Edit, Text** command to paste the picture in its permanent position on the card, as shown on the next page.

Colour pictures are converted into black & white when transferred onto a card.

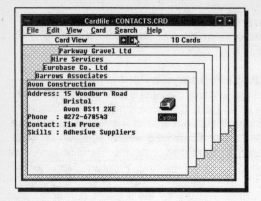

If a picture is larger than the available area on the card, only that part of it that can fit in the available area will be displayed; use the arrow keys to select a part of the picture which is not shown on the card, before pasting it permanently with the **Edit, Text** command.

Warning: Do not be tempted to paste large pictures, unless your system contains at least 4 MB of memory. If you do, you might find that you are unable to retrieve these particular record cards in your database. To overcome this problem, delete the offending cards and re-enter the information. A backup copy of your database is absolutely invaluable.

Embedding a Picture into Cardfile:
Embedding a picture or a drawing into Cardfile is similar to copying, but with one important advantage: You can actually edit an embedded object, because you can open Paintbrush from within Cardfile.

Obviously, you can only use other applications in place of Cardfile and Paintbrush to embed pictures or drawings, if these applications are capable of supporting embedding.

To embed a Paintbrush drawing into Cardfile, transfer the drawing from Paintbrush onto the Clipboard, as detailed previously under 'Copying and Pasting a Picture on a Card', then use the **Edit, Paste** command from within Cardfile.

Linking a Picture into Cardfile:
The advantage of linking files dynamically is that it allows information held in one file to be automatically updated when the information in the other file changes.

To link a Paintbrush drawing into Cardfile, transfer it from Paintbrush to the Clipboard, then use the **Edit, Link** command from within Cardfile.

Printing a Cardfile Database

You can print either a single record from a Cardfile database or the entire file.

- To print a single record, make it the current record and then select the **File, Print** command,

- To print the records of an entire file, select the **File, Print All** command.

When printing, Cardfile uses the default margin settings in the Page Setup dialogue box. You can change these by selecting the **File, Page Setup** command.

7. THE WINDOWS CALENDAR

The Windows Calendar lets you organise your time by allowing you to fill in and see at a glance a month-by-month calendar and a daily appointments book. Switching between the two is made extremely easy and you can even set up early warnings for vital appointments.

To start Calendar, double-click at its icon in the Accessories group of programs, which causes the following untitled screen to be displayed:

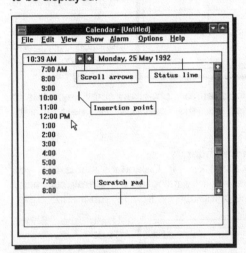

This screen is divided into several areas, with the current date and time being displayed in the 'status line', below the usual menu bar. If the time and/or date is not correct, then exit the Calendar, activate the Control Panel and use the Date/Time option to change the system date and time.

In the middle of Calendar's screen there is an area for entering appointments (up to 80 characters long), next to a default column of times, starting with 7.00 a.m. At the bottom of the screen, there is another area, called 'scratch pad' in which you can enter lengthier reminders (up to three lines long). Clicking at the scroll arrows, in the middle of the status line, causes Calendar to display the previous and next day, respectively.

Calendar's Two Views

Calendar has two views; the day-view which is the default starting view, and the month-view which can be displayed by selecting the **View**, **Month** command, or by double-clicking on the date in the status line. The result is displayed overleaf:

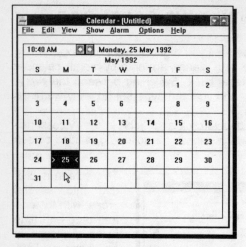

To return to the day-view display, simply select the **V**iew, **D**ay command, or double-click the highlighted date on the month-view. If you prefer to use the keyboard, you can go from a day-view to a month-view by pressing the **F9** function key, and back again by pressing **F8**.

Pressing the status line's left- or right-arrow scroll key, while in the month-view, displays the previous or next month, respectively.

Navigating Through Calendar:
Apart from using the scroll keys in Calendar's status line, you can find your way around it by selecting the **S**how command and then choosing one of the options from its sub-menu.

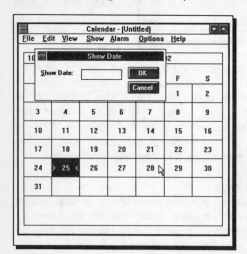

Using the **S**how, **T**oday command, displays the current day-view or highlights the current day in the month-view. Selecting the **P**revious or **N**ext option from the sub-menu, displays the previous or next day's calendar (if in day-view), or the previous or next month's calendar (if in month-view).

To display a specific date, use the **Show, Date** command (or press the **F4** function key) which causes the dialogue box shown on the previous page to appear on your screen.

Attempting to enter a date in any but the dd/mm/yy format, causes Calendar to display a warning dialogue box telling you how you should enter a date. Entering, say, 1/6/91 will display either the day-view for 1 June, 1991 or highlight that day in the month-view, depending in which view you are in at the time.

Changing Calendar's Settings:

When you activate Calendar for the first time, and if you are a U.K. user, the day-view displays a 24-hour column of times starting at 7.00 a.m. in increments of 60 minutes. These options can be changed by using the **Options, Day Settings** command which causes the following dialogue box to be displayed:

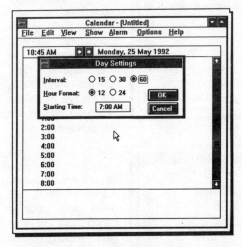

From here, you can change the displayed time interval down to 30 or 15 minutes from the default value of 60 minutes, or change the hour format from the default 24-hour display to a 12-hour display, or change the starting time of Calendar's day-view display. This starting time option has to do with the display only; times earlier than 7.00 a.m. can be brought into view by using the scroll bar on the right-hand side of Calendar's display. In fact, Calendar's appointment times start at 0:00 and end at 23:00 in a 24-hour format, or 12:00 (mid-night) and end 11:00 p.m. in a 12-hour format.

Entering Appointments

Calendar allows you to organise your time effectively with an at-a-glance month-view of how this time is to be spent.

To start with, let us type in two appointments for meetings; one for 10:00 a.m. on 3 June, the other for the same time a week later. To do so, double-click on 3 June on the month-view to switch to the day-view, move the cursor to 10:00 a.m. and type 'Managers' meeting'. Then move to the scratch pad (either point and click the mouse button or press the <Tab> key) and add the reminder 'Allow 2 hours for meeting', as shown below:

One way of repeating the same entries in the diary for 10 June is to highlight in turn the entries in the 3 June day-view, and use the **Edit, Copy** command, followed by the **Edit, Paste** command, having first navigated to the required date via the month-view. Of course, for short entries retyping will be quicker.

Further, let us assume that you also have a special lunch appointment with your mother on 3 June, as it is her birthday. Enter this information in the day-view by typing against 1:00 p.m. 'Lunch with mother', as shown, and add on the scratch pad the reminder 'Birthday lunch'.

Note, however, that when in month-view display, information on the scratch pad is only visible, if the day that contains it is highlighted (3 June in our case). When any other day is highlighted, there is no indication whatsoever that you might have appointments on any other days of the month.

Marking an Active Date
A date can be marked as active by selecting the **Options, Mark** command (or pressing **F6**), which causes the adjacent dialogue box to be displayed.

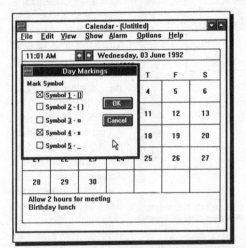

It is here that you can specify which of five symbols you want to assign to the active date - you can assign more than one. You could, for example choose to mark a date with Symbol 1 to indicate business meetings, Symbol 2 to indicate personal meetings, Symbol 3 to indicate business lunches, Symbol 4 to indicate special lunches, and so on.

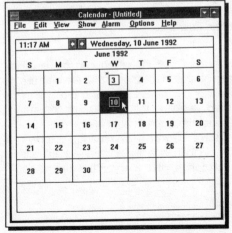

In our example, since on 3 June we have a business meeting and a special lunch, we choose to mark the date with Symbols 1 & 4 by clicking at the boxes adjacent to them. Pressing the **OK** button produces the display opposite.

Note that now, you can tell at-a-glance what sort of meetings you have during the whole of the month.

Adding Special Times

Let us suppose that you have just been informed that your meeting of 3 June has been moved to 3:10 p.m. from its previous morning slot.

To add a special time into Calendar's day-view, select the **Options, Special Time** command and type the required time in the displayed dialogue box, not forgetting to specify a.m. or p.m. if you are operating in 12-hour format. On the adjacent screen, we show the day view with the Special Time dialogue box, as well as the inserted time which will be displayed after you have pressed the **Insert** button of the dialogue box. The appointment message was subsequently moved to the new time.

Setting an Alarm

Calendar has a special alarm feature which can be used to remind you, in advance, of important meetings. An alarm can be set against a specific appointment by moving the cursor to that appointment and then selecting the **Alarm, Set** command. A small bell appears against the appropriate time.

Now selecting the **Alarm, Control** command, displays a dialogue box in which you can specify an 'early ring' option and/or change the 'sound' option, as shown on the next page.

When an alarm goes off, Calendar alerts you either by displaying a dialogue box if Calendar is active, or by causing the title bar at the top of Calendar to flash if Calendar is inactive, or by flashing Calendar's icon if the Accessories group is visible. If you clear the 'sound' check box, then no audible sound will accompany the alarm.

Once the alarm goes off, it will continue to flash and beep until you turn it off. To do so, activate Calendar if it is not already active, and when the warning dialogue box appears, press the **OK** button.

Calendar Keystrokes

Working with Calendar can be keyboard intensive. Thus mixing typing with mouse movements can become unproductive. Below we list several keystrokes which can be used to quickly accomplish certain results. These are:

Keystroke	*Result*
F4	Show particular date
F5	Set appointment alarm
F6	Mark a date
F7	Insert/Delete special time
F8	Switch to day-view
F9	Switch to month-view
Ctrl+Ins	Edit, Copy (or Ctrl+C)
Ctrl+PgUp	Show previous day/month
Ctrl+PgDn	Show next day/month
Shift+Del	Edit, Cut (or Ctrl+X)
Shift+Ins	Edit, Paste (or Ctrl+V)

Calendar's Files & Reports

You can create and manage several different Calendar files, such as a business calendar, a personal calendar, etc. All you need to do is save each created calendar under a separate name using the **File, Save As** command - the program adds automatically the extension .CAL to the filename.

You can even print your appointment schedule by selecting the appropriate Calendar file and then selecting the **File, Print** command which causes the Print dialogue box to appear. Here you have the option to print all your appointments from the current date (offered as default) to any date you care to specify.

As with other Windows modules, you can set-up a print page to have the margins of your choice, and you can arrange for your printouts to have headers and footers. You can even include the following codes in a header or footer:

Code	Result
&d	Enter current date
&f	Enter current filename
&p	Enter current page
&t	Enter current time
&c	Centre the text that follows
&l	Left justify the text that follows
&r	Right justify the text that follows.

Any or all of the above codes can be included in a single header or footer.

* * *

Calendar provides you with an effective time-management tool, if only you use it regularly. Perhaps, in order to benefit from its time-saving capability, you must find the time to use it!

8. THE WINDOWS TERMINAL

The Terminal module allows you to (a) connect your computer to another which is situated in the same room, and (b) connect your computer to other computers which are in different locations so that you can interchange information. You could, for example, search a library catalogue, browse through the offerings of a bulletin board, or send and receive Email.

To connect your computer to another computer in the same room, all you need is a cable called a 'null modem cable' to connect the two machines via their serial (COM) ports, and a copy of Terminal (although another similar type of program could do just as well) on each computer.

To connect your computer to computers located at different places, you need a 'modem', a cable to connect to your telephone socket, and Terminal (or a similar communications type program). However, before you can connect to an outside service, you need to know their communications settings. For example, you need to know the settings for 'baud rate', 'data bits', 'stop bits', 'parity', and 'flow control method', although most of these can be safely assumed to be the same as the default values offered by terminal. Finally, before you can make the connection, you might need to know a password or two, as most services are not free.

Starting Terminal

You can activate Terminal by double-clicking at its icon in the Accessories group of programs. If this is the first time that Terminal is being accessed from the particular computer, Windows requests information regarding your system's configuration relating to the usage of its serial communication ports (COM1, COM2, etc.) by displaying the following message:

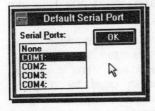

If you do have a modem, look up its reference manual which will tell you to which port the modem is connected and select the appropriate port on the dialogue box. If, on the other hand, you do not have a modem, but you would like to explore Terminal, choose the

'None' option in the dialogue box which will allow you to look at the various options available. Selecting this option, however, bars you from accessing a remote computer service.

Setting Communication Parameters

You can specify all the necessary communication parameters required for a successful connection by selecting the **Settings** command from Terminal's menu bar, which when selected produces the following pull-down sub-menu:

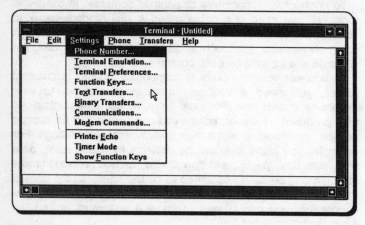

It is from here that you can set the various communication parameters so that the two connected computers can understand each other. We shall examine what each one of these necessary parameters means by looking at the **Terminal Emulation**, **Terminal Preferences**, **Communications** and **Phone Number** options of the **Settings** sub-menu.

Specifying Terminal Emulation:

On selecting the **Terminal Emulation** option, the following dialogue box appears on your screen:

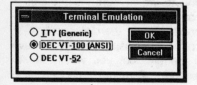

The word 'terminal' here, refers to the type of keyboard and display screen used by a given computer. By allowing a computer to emulate one of

98

three possible terminal emulations, unlike computers can be made to look alike. Your choice depends on what type of computer or service you are trying to connect to.

The Windows Terminal program allows you to specify easily one of three terminal emulations so that the remote system can understand the formatting codes sent to it. These are:

Type of Connection	*Used For*
DEC VT-100 (ANSI)	The default choice which is also used for connecting to other PCs or an external on-line service
DEC VT-52	Used mainly to connect to mainframe computers
TTY (Generic)	Used if everything else fails; with this emulation, the remote system receives formatting codes for carriage return, backspace, and tab characters only.

Specifying Terminal Preferences:

By selecting the **Terminal Preferences** option, you can specify how your terminal performs during a communications session,

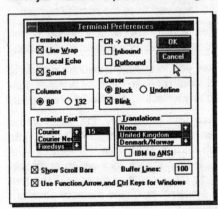

in terms of how it should handle information sent to it by the remote computer. On selecting this option, the adjacent dialogue box appears on your screen.

The terminal preferences you can select in this dialogue box are discussed fully on the next page.

Option	Result
Line Wrap	Automatically formats incoming information to fit within the column width selected for your terminal (see 'Columns' in dialogue box).
Local Echo	Displays the data you are sending to the remote computer on your screen, as you are typing it on your keyboard.
Sound	Activate or deactivates the warning beep for the remote computer.
Columns	Allows you to specify the display width in which Terminal should format data.
Terminal Font	Allows you to select any of the fonts installed by Windows for use by Terminal.
Show Scroll Bars	Allows you to review information you have already typed but has scrolled out of view.
CR or CR/LF	Allows you to specify whether Terminal should add a line feed to each carriage return received from the remote system.
Cursor	Allows you to specify the shape of the cursor and whether it should blink or not.
Translation	Allows you to specify a country setting to send and receive data in another language by selecting another character set.
Buffer Lines	Allows you to specify the size of the buffer, ranging from 25 to 400 lines, into which data is sent from the remote system. Terminal sets this option automatically to the largest number of lines that your system's available memory permits.

Specifying Communications Settings:

Selecting the **Communications** option, allows you to configure your system so that it speaks the same language as the remote system. On activating the option, the following dialogue box appears on your screen.

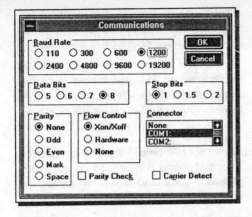

If the options within the dialogue box are dimmed, select **COM1:** from the 'Connector' field at the bottom right-hand side of the dialogue box. This will allow you to see them clearly.

Normally, you will find that the default parameters in this dialogue box are the ones you would want to use. However, in case you need to change them, we list below their meaning and usage.

Option	*Result*
Baud Rate	Allows you to specify the transmission rate at which your system sends and receives data. The type of modem attached to your system determines the rate.
Data Bits	Allows you to specify the number of data bits (binary digits) that each data packet, sent or received, contains.
Stop Bits	Allows you to specify the time between transmitted characters.
Parity	Allows you to specify how the receiving computer verifies the accuracy of the data you are sending.
Flow Control	Allows you to specify what Terminal should do if its buffer fills up during data reception. Xon/Xoff tells Terminal to pause when the buffer fills, and to send a message to the remote system when ready to receive more data.
Connector	Allows you to specify the communications port used by your system's modem.

101

Parity Check	Allows you to activate the option of letting Terminal display the byte in which any parity check errors have occurred.
Carrier Detect	Allows you to tell Terminal to use the modem signal for determining a carrier signal, if on. Turn this option on if you have a 100% Hayes compatible modem.

Specifying a Phone Number:

The last thing you need to specify before making connection with a remote system is its telephone number. To do so, select the **Settings, Phone Number** command which will cause the following dialogue box to appear on your screen:

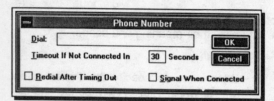

It is here that you enter the number which Terminal is to 'Dial'. Other options in the dialogue box have the following meaning:

Option	Result
Timeout	Specifies the time Terminal is to wait for a successful connection to be made.
Redial	When activated causes Terminal to automatically try to redial, if connection is not successful within the time specified in 'Timeout'.
Signal	When activated causes Terminal to beep once a connection is successful.

Saving Settings to Disc:

Once all settings and options have been set, you can use the **File, Save As** command to save them to disc so that in future you only need to load such a file into memory to have it prepare terminal for the remote connection. Terminal adds the extension **.trm** automatically to the typed filename.

102

Preparing Files for Transfer

Before you can send or receive files using Terminal's **Transfers** command, you need to specify the transfer settings. You only need to do this if you intend to send or receive text or binary files. You don't need to do any of what follows if you only intend to read or send electronic mail.

Text files: are normally prepared with a text editor or a word processor, such as Write or Notepad, but saved unformatted. This means that files are save in ASCII format with only a few formatting codes such as carriage returns and linefeeds.

Binary files: are normally program files which contain characters from both the ASCII and the extended ASCII character sets.

Text File Transfer Preparation:

To prepare for a text file transfer, select the **Settings, Text Transfers** command which produces the following dialogue box:

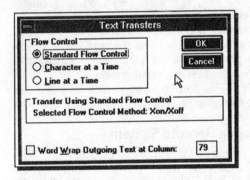

Choose the default **Standard Flow Control** option if you want to select the flow control method specified with the **Communications** option of the **Settings** command. The remaining two options are selected only if delays between characters or lines are required in order to slow down the transfer process and thus minimise errors.

Binary File Transfer Preparation:

Binary files are normally transferred using standard protocols for data transmission, but you must specify the protocol used by the remote system. To prepare for binary file transfer, select the **Settings, Binary Transfers** command which produces the following dialogue box:

Selecting the **XModem/CRC** protocol tells Terminal to use all 8

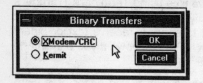

bits as data bits, which requires the Parity option to be set to None (use the **Settings, Communications** command to set the Parity). Selecting the **Kermit** protocol tells Terminal to use either 7 or 8 bits as data bits, which requires the Parity to be specified as Even, Odd, or None (the last setting for 8 data bits).

Connecting to a Remote System

To connect to a remote system, use the **File, Open** command and load into memory the appropriate Terminal settings file (previously specified and saved to disc) for the particular remote service. Then select the **Phone, Dial** command to start dialling the remote system.

Once connection to the remote system is successfully made, use the **Transfers** command and then select an appropriate option from the drop-down sub-menu.

Selecting one of the four options for sending/receiving data, causes an appropriate dialogue box to be displayed from which you load an already prepared file for sending, or specify the name of a file into which to receive incoming data.

The option **View Text File** can be used to look at a text file either before sending it or after receiving it.

Disconnecting from a Remote System

After you have sent or received information from a remote system, disconnect by selecting the **Phone, Hangup** command.

However, do note that with some services you must first sign off before disconnecting Terminal. If you don't sign off, you will continue to be billed for on-line services, even though you are disconnected from that service!

9. OTHER APPLICATIONS

The Notepad

Notepad is a text editor which you can use to write short memos, or create and edit batch files. You can use Notepad to read text files such as the various .TXT files supplied with Windows.

To see Notepad in operation, double-click at its icon in the Accessories group of programs, then select the **File, Open** command and double-click at the filename **setup.txt**. You should have the following on your screen:

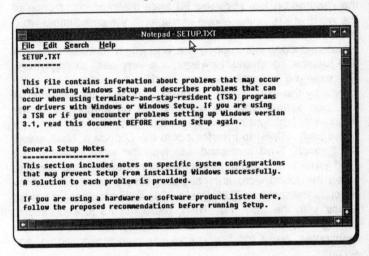

It is worth reading the above opening screen, particularly if you are experiencing difficulties while running SETUP or while running Windows with TSRs (terminate-and-stay-resident) programs.

Notepad's Edit Features:

Although Notepad is not as powerful as Write, it nevertheless has some interesting features, such as the ability to turn on word wrap which causes words that will not fit within its page margins to be placed on the next line automatically. You can turn word wrap on by selecting the **Edit, Word Wrap** command.

Another Notepad feature is the **Select All** option from the **Files** menu which allows you to highlight a whole document at a stroke in order to, say, copy it onto the Clipboard.

Notepad supports the usual edit features which are useful when working with files, such as cut, copy, paste, and delete, all of which are options of the **Edit** menu.

Searching for Text:

You can even use Notepad to search and find text, by selecting the **Search, Find** command. Typing the word 'press' and pressing the **OK** button, will find the first occurrence of the word in the middle of the first line of the second bullet paragraph of the **readme.txt** file. Pressing **F3** finds the next occurrence of the word which, in the above example, is the penultimate word of the last displayed line.

Notepad does not support the equivalent to Write's 'search and replace' command. However, it is very easy to implement. For example, suppose you would like to replace the word 'press' by the word 'hit' in the opening page of the **readme.txt** file, then simply type the word 'hit' on an empty line of the document, highlight it, and select the **Edit, Cut** command (or press Shift+<Del>) to transfer it onto the Clipboard. Next, select the **Search, Find** command and type the word 'press' in the **Find** What box. Pressing the **OK** button searches the text and when the found word is highlighted, simply press Shift+<Ins> which is the same as **Edit, Paste**. This action replaces the word 'press' with the word 'hit'. Then, press the **F3** function key to highlight the next occurrence of the word 'press' and, when it is highlighted, press the Shift+<Ins> key combination again, and so on.

Creating a Log File:

If you have to account how you spend your time, say because you have to charge someone for it, you could use Notepad as an effective time keeper, provided you were running a Windows version other than 3.0. Even though the manual tells you how you can use Windows 3.0 to log time, you will not be able to do it because there is a bug in the program that prevents you from using it effectively; the accessory under Windows 3.0 is only capable of logging the date, not both time and date, which makes it rather ineffective.

However, this bug has been fixed in version 3.1 of the program, and it is worth describing. To create a time-log, type .LOG on the first line, as near to the left margin as you possibly can, in an untitled Notepad screen; the period and the use of uppercase letters is important. Next, use the **File, Save As** command and save this screen under the filename **timelog**. The program will add the **.txt** extension.

From now on, every time you open the file **timelog.txt,** the current time and date will appear automatically on an empty line, as follows:

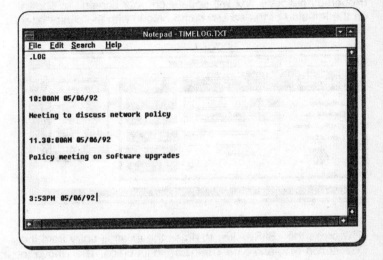

Thus, every time you are about to start some new activity, all you need to do is open Notepad and type an appropriate message under the offered Time/Date stamp.

Automating the Time-log Process:
As it stands now, whenever you want to log a new activity you will have to double-click on the Notepad icon, then select the **File, Open** command, and double-click on the **timelog.txt** file. This is rather a laborious method, therefore we will seek to automated it. The technique requires you to transfer Notepad's icon into the Utilities group of programs which we created at the beginning of Chapter 3.

If you haven't already created the Utilities group of programs, then you will need to create it now; it will only take you a minute to do so. Then proceed to copy the Notepad icon from the Accessories group of programs into the Utilities group of programs by pointing to the Notepad icon, pressing the Ctrl key and while keeping it down, press the left mouse button and drag the icon into the Utilities group.

Next, click on the Notepad icon in the Utilities group to make it the active icon, and select the **File**, **Properties** command from the Program Manager's menu bar. The Program Item Properties dialogue box will appear on your screen, as shown on the left-side of the screen dump below, with the cursor after the entry **Notepad** in the **D**escription box.

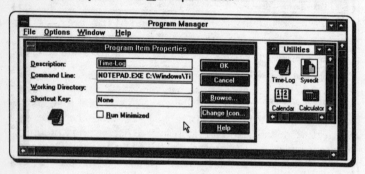

Now press the <BkSp> key to erase the existing entry from the **D**escription box, and type **Time-Log** in its place. Then move to the **C**ommand Line box, place the cursor at the end of the existing entry NOTEPAD.EXE, press the spacebar to insert a space after it and type **C:\Windows\timelog.txt**. Of course, this assumes that the file **timelog.txt** exists and is saved under the **Windows** directory in the C: drive. On pressing the **OK** button, the Notepad icon in the Utilities group of programs acquires the name **Time-Log**, as shown on the right-side of the above screen dump.

From now on, double-clicking on the **Time-Log** icon in the Utilities group of programs, causes this application to start, but with the **timelog.txt** file opened automatically, ready for a new entry.

The Macro Recorder

A macro is a sequence of instructions, made up of keystrokes and commands that you normally would have typed onto the keyboard and/or selected with the mouse. This sequence of keystrokes and commands can be recorded by the Windows accessory Recorder for future use in order to help save time in performing repetitive actions.

To create a macro, you need to perform the following steps:

- Activate the Recorder and give information on the intended macro by filling the displayed Record Macro dialogue box (including your choice of name and a shortcut key to be used later for the purpose of activating it), and start the Recorder.

- Activate the application you intend to use to create the macro, create the sequence of keystrokes and/or mouse selections which will constitute the macro, switch off the macro Recorder, and save the macro.

To illustrate the above process, we will create a simple macro of a fictitious office address, which can be used later to replicate the information at a touch of a key. To start the process, double-click at the Recorder icon in the Accessories group of programs which will cause the display of an untitled Recorder window. Now select the **Macro, Record** command which displays the following dialogue box:

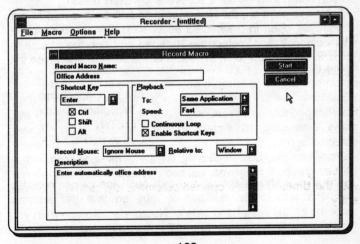

The Record Options:

Whenever you create a new macro the Record Macro dialogue box appears on you screen. Different macros might require different choices to be selected from the various record options. For example, you can choose such things as:

* The shortcut key and which of three other keys can be used with it to activate the macro.

* Play back the macro only in the application where it was recorded or play back in all applications.

* Play back quickly or at the recorded speed.

* Record mouse movements relative to only a window, or the whole screen.

* Record mouse movements and keystrokes, or keystrokes only.

These options can be selected by clicking at the down-arrows displayed next to the relevant field boxes which produce lists of alternative options to the displayed standard settings.

Returning to our example, type 'Office Address' in the Record Macro Name field of the Record Macro dialogue box, select 'Enter' for the Shortcut Key field, select 'Ignore Mouse' for the Record Mouse field, and type 'Enter automatically office address' in the Description field, as shown in the previous screen dump. Having done so, press the **Start** button.

From this point on, the Recorder is on and it will record all our keystrokes once in a selected application. For the purpose of this demonstration, select the Notepad and use the mouse to expand the window to fill the width of the screen. Then type the address:

ADEPT Consultants
1 Woodland Avenue
PENRYN
Cornwall TR99 77XZ

Tel: 0326-335577

in the format shown above, and with each line being preceded with the appropriate number of tabs so that the address appears on the right hand side of Notepad's screen. When you finish, press Ctrl+<Break> to end the macro recording.

What now appears on your screen is the following dialogue box:

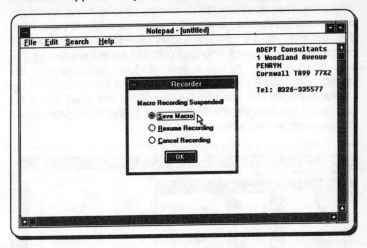

To save your macro, select the <u>S</u>ave Macro button in the Recorder dialogue box and press the **OK** button.

From now on, whenever you open the Notepad accessory you can insert your office address by simply using the Ctrl+<Enter> keystroke. Try it, it is fascinating watching the macro execute every single keystroke, including your errors and subsequent corrections!

Using Macros in Demos:
You could use the Recorder to put together a demonstration of an application and have it play back at an appropriate slow speed so that the audience can see what is happening. You could even set a demonstration to run in a continuous loop until you turn off the computer.

Obviously, to achieve such results, you must practice with simple macros first. However, for best results avoid using excessive mouse movements within a macro because, as you must have noticed by now, application windows do not always open the same size on screen and the mouse pointer might be pointing at something different than the intended place. For example, avoid using the mouse to choose menu options while recording a macro; use the keyboard shortcut keys instead.

The PIF Editor

When you run standard DOS programs under the Windows environment, Windows looks for a corresponding filename with the **.pif** extension in the **Windows** directory. A PIF file is a custom file put there during SETUP, and contains settings that tells Windows how to run a non-Windows application. If the application's **.pif** file can not be found, then Windows uses the **_default.pif** file (the underline is part of the filename). Either file can be edited with the PIF Editor to be found in the Main group of programs, shown below:

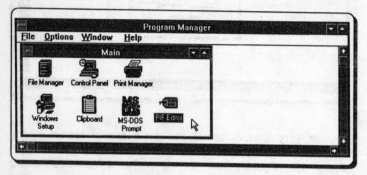

Changing the PIF Settings:

Changing the PIF settings can affect how and whether an application runs under Windows. Each PIF contains two sets of options; the standard option for running the application in Standard mode, and the 386 Enhanced option for running the application in 386 Enhanced mode.

Before going on, make sure you have one standard DOS program set up as a Non-Windows Application. If you have not, double-click at the **Windows Setup** icon of the Main group of applications, then click at the **Options** option, and select **Set Up Applications** from the revealed sub-menu. Next, specify the drive where your DOS application is to be found and let the SETUP program find it for you. It will also find all sorts of other programs, but select one you are familiar with, and **Add** it to your Windows environment. We have chosen here to use Q&A (an integrated database and word processor package), as an example. You, of course, follow the steps we suggest, but use the DOS package of your choice.

Double-clicking at the PIF Editor icon displays the following screen:

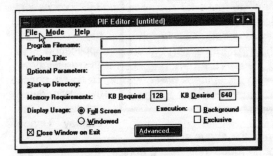

To see what type of information you will have to give to PIF Editor, use the **File, Open** command from its menu bar. The following File Open dialogue box is displayed on your screen:

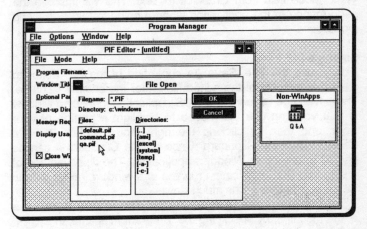

If you only have one program in your Non-Windows Application group (we have shortened the group's name to 'NonWinApps', you will only see two **.pif** files listed in the dialogue box; the **_default.pif** and your application's **.pif** (here this is **qa.pif**). In the above display there is a third PIF which will be discussed later.

Next, select your application's PIF and press the **OK** button. This causes information about the selected file to be transferred to the PIF Editor screen, as shown overleaf.

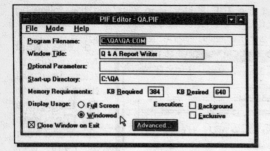

If your have a computer with a 386 processor, then you could run your DOS application in its own window. To do so, check the Windowed option of the Display Usage field at the bottom of the above screen.

If your application does not use graphics, then press the **Advanced** button and make sure you change the option of the **V**ideo Mode field from Graphics to Text. This will improve the performance of the application when running in 386 Enhanced mode.

Saving a PIF File:

Finally, use the **F**ile, Save **A**s command of the PIF Editor to save the contents of the edited file under the original filename. The advantage of running a DOS application in its own window is that you can use the mouse to highlight a portion of your work, and then by clicking the right mouse button, have it transferred to the Clipboard. Once on the Clipboard it can be pasted to any other Windows application. The disadvantage of a standard DOS application running in a window, rather than in full screen, is that it runs much slower.

You can even force DOS to run in its own window, if you have a 386 machine, by specifying the 'Program Filename' in the PIF Editor as **c:\command.com**, and the 'Window Title' as **DOS Prompt**, with the 'Start-up Directory' as **c:**, and check-marking the 'Windowed' option. From then on, whenever you click at the **DOS Prompt** icon of the Main group of applications, DOS will be run in its own window. To exit from DOS, type EXIT at the C:\> prompt.

The Calculator

The Windows Calculator has two faces; the ordinary calculator that can add, subtract. multiply, divide, take the square root of a number, find its reciprocal, or find a percentage of it, and the scientific calculator which much more powerful.

Starting the Calculator:

To start the Calculator, double-click at its icon in the Accessory group of programs. Normally, the standard view of Calculator appears on your screen, as follows:

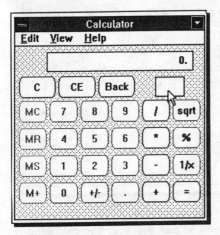

If, however, you have activated Calculator at a previous occasion and changed its view to that of the scientific one, then that view will be what is displayed on your screen. To use the calculator, you could either type the numbers and arithmetic operators on the keyboard, or use the mouse to point and click at the numbers and operators displayed on the calculator screen. Obviously, if you wish to find the inverse of a number or its square root, you must use the Calculator keys as these operators are not on your keyboard.

The Calculator's Memory:

Calculator has four memory keys situated on the left-side of the screen. Going from top to bottom, their functions is as follows:

Key	Function
MC	Clears memory of stored values
MR	Recalls stored values from memory to display
MS	Stores the current displayed value in memory
M+	Adds the display value to a value in memory.

The Scientific Calculator:

You can access the scientific calculator by selecting the **V**iew, **S**cien**t**ific command from Calculator's menu bar. What appears on your screen now is rather more complicated looking, as shown below:

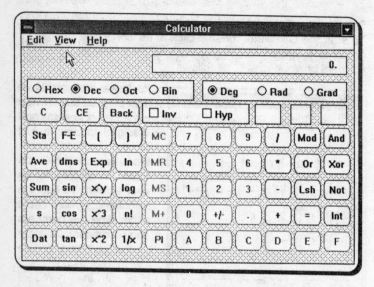

Obviously you will only need to use the scientific calculator if you already know how to use one. For this very reason we will not waste space and time explaining extremely complicated mathematical concepts

Using Calculator with Clipboard:

You can transfer the results of any calculation appearing on the Calculator's display to the Clipboard by selecting the **E**dit, **C**opy command.

Once results have been copied to the Clipboard, you can now paste them into any Windows application by selecting the **E**dit, **P**aste command of the relevant application.

APPENDIX A

Fine Tuning Windows

When you first installed Windows, the SETUP program created or amended the **config.sys** and **autoexec.bat** files in your system's root directory of the C: drive. You could get Windows to perform more efficiently by slightly changing the contents of these files - as both are text files you can change them with DOS' screen editor **Edit** or any text editor, including Windows' Notepad and Sysedit.

However, what changes you make to these files so as to optimize your system, depends on the type of processor in your computer (Intel 80286 or Intel 80386 and higher), the version of the operating system (DOS 3.3 or 5.0), and the type and size of extra RAM memory available in your system.

To successfully optimize your system's resources (a balance between speed of execution of applications and maximizing available conventional memory), you need to understand how your computer manages its memory. In general, the more memory you have, the more application programs you can run simultaneously. There are four types of memory available:

Conventional   the first 640 Kbytes of your system's memory. How this is managed depends on the type of processor in your computer and the version of MS-DOS.

Extended   the memory on your system beyond 1 Mbyte on 80286 (or higher) processors. Windows requires extended memory to run and also requires the HIMEM extended memory-manager. The 384 Kbytes above the 640 Kbytes is referred to as the 'upper memory area'.

Expanded   the memory that comes on expanded memory boards. This type of memory can only be used by Windows if it is configured as extended memory.

Virtual   the space used on your hard disc by Windows to 'swap files'. This type of memory allows more programs to run simultaneously, but is very slow.

You will see from what follows that, if you want to get the best out of Windows and the application programs running under it, you must seriously consider upgrading your operating system to MS-DOS 5.0, as this version of the operating system can free more conventional memory which can be used by Windows and which can speed up program execution. The most efficient way of optimizing Windows is to configure your computer's memory correctly.

Memory Management of MS-DOS 5

On computers with Intel's 80286 or higher processor, DOS 5 loads itself in extended memory (the memory beyond 1 Mbyte, freeing at least 45 Kbytes of conventional memory (the first 640 Kbytes of RAM), for your program applications. The extended memory (including the first 64 Kbytes above the 1 Mbyte) known as HMA - the High Memory Area, is managed by HIGHMEM.SYS, while the conventional memory is managed by a DOS built-in memory manager using MCBs (Memory Control Blocks).

A pictorial view of how memory is managed on a typical 80286 computer when using MS-DOS 3.3, and what happens when MS-DOS 5 is used in conjunction with the **DOS=HIGH** command in the **config.sys** file, is shown below:

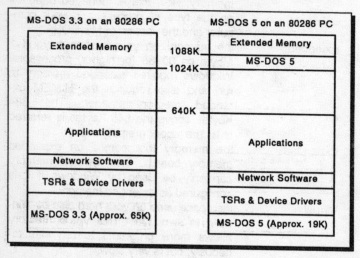

On computers with Intel's more advanced 80386 (or higher) processor, you can load device drivers, TSR (Terminate and Stay Resident) programs, and network software drivers into 'upper' memory (the memory between 640 Kbytes and 1024 Mbytes). The chunks of memory available to the user, between the various hardware-dependent ROMs and the video memory, is managed by UMBs (Upper Memory Blocks) and access to these is governed by the EMM386.EXE utility, thus freeing even more space in conventional memory for running application programs.

Unfortunately, the 32 Kbyte video ROM splits the free area in upper memory into two sections, a lower area of 32 Kbytes and a higher area of 96 Kbytes. In addition, the 64 Kbyte BIOS ROM sits in the segment just below the 1 Mbyte position. Thus, what you load in upper memory, and where (i.e. in what order), depends on the size of the files you are loading. For this reason, MS-DOS leaves this bit of fine tuning entirely to the user.

The corresponding pictorial view of how memory is managed on a typical 80386 computer when using MS-DOS 3.3, and what happens when MS-DOS 5 is used in conjunction with the **DEVICE=EMM386.EXE** and **DOS=HIGH, UMB** commands in the **config.sys** file (more about this later), is shown below:

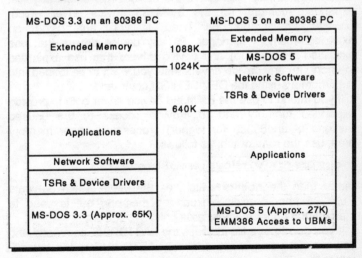

If you have an 80386 (or higher) processor system with extended memory and you need to run programs that make use of expanded memory, then you can install the EMM386.EXE device driver that can use extended memory to provide expanded memory.

The fine tuning of loading the maximum number of device drivers into upper memory can be done by trial and error, by finding out the size of the various blocks with the use of the **MEM /C** command and loading the required device drivers in the available memory blocks with the use of the **DEVICEHIGH=** command in the **autoexec.bat** file.

Increasing Conventional Memory:
To install HIMEM and run DOS in extended memory so as to free more conventional memory, when using Windows 3.1, use **Edit** or Sysedit to open your **config.sys** file and check that the following lines appear near the beginning of the file:

```
device=c:\windows\himem.sys
dos=high,umb
```

Following the above entries, the optimum order in which your **config.sys** file should start device drivers is: (a) the expanded-memory manager if the system has actual physical expanded memory, (b) the EMM386 device driver which, however, must not be used if you are using an expanded-memory manager, (c) any device drivers that use extended memory, (d) any device drivers that use expanded memory, (e) any device drivers that you want to be loaded into high memory using the DEVICEHIGH command.

If you intend to use the EMM386 device driver both to provide expanded memory and to provide access to the unused portions of an 80386 (or higher) processor's upper memory area, use the **ram** switch, as follows:

```
device=c:\windows\emm386.exe ram
```

rather than the **noems** switch, as the latter switch prevents EMM386 from providing expanded memory, but is used to manage the upper memory area only.

If you **config.sys** file includes the LASTDRIVE command and you are not using a network, set LASTDRIVE to the letter E rather than Z, as each letter uses up about 100 bytes more than the preceding one. However, on systems with more than 1 Mbyte of memory, the saving that this provides is outweighed by the inflexibility introduced in not being able to use the SUBST command effectively, which associates a path with a drive letter.

Speeding up Your System:
To speed up program execution, use the BUFFERS command in your **config.sys** file to increase the number of buffers (up to 50, depending on the hard disc size) MS-DOS is using for file transfer. The more buffers the faster your system works, but it also uses more memory.

The most effective buffer sizes are: 20 for a hard-disc size of less than 40 Mbytes, 30 for a hard-disc drive between 40 and 79 Mbytes, 40 for a hard-disc drive between 80 and 119 Mbytes, and 50 for hard-disc drives in excess of 120 Mbytes. The command takes the form:

```
buffers=40
```

Another way of speeding up your system is to use the RAMDrive memory-disc program in your **config.sys** file. The appropriate command is:

```
device=c:\dos\ramdrive.sys 512 /e
```

The command allows you to use part of your system's memory (512 Kbytes in this case), to emulate a very fast, but temporary disc drive which resides in extended RAM (specified by the switch /e). However, because information resides in RAM, it is lost unless you copy it onto the hard disc before you switch off your system. One possible use of a RAM drive is to use it as the TEMP environment variable so that programs which require to write temporary files to disc can use the RAM drive instead. To do this, use the following command within your **autoexec.bat** file

```
set TEMP=d:\
```

and since such programs delete temporary files after use, you'll not have to worry about losing information. Use uppercase letters for TEMP as many programs do not recognise the environment variable if written in lower case.

Another way of speeding up your system is with the use of the SMARTDrive disc caching program. Prior to Windows 3.1, but with DOS 5.0, this was achieved by loading the program as a device driver from within the **config.sys** file. With Windows 3.1, this is now done from within the **autoexec.bat** file with the

```
c:\windows\smartdrv.exe
```

command which SETUP inserts for you automatically into the **autoexec.bat** file after deleting any reference to SMARTDrive from your **config.sys** file.

The Config.sys File

Thus, taking into consideration all the points raised so far, your **config.sys** file for a 386 (or higher) processor could contain the following commands:

```
SHELL=C:\DOS\COMMAND.COM C:\DOS\ /E:256 /P
DEVICE=C:\WINDOWS\HIMEM.SYS
DOS=HIGH,UMB
DEVICE=C:\WINDOWS\EMM386.EXE RAM
DEVICEHIGH=C:\WINDOWS\RAMDRIVE.SYS 512 /E
DEVICE=C:\DOS\ANSI.SYS
COUNTRY=044,,C:\DOS\COUNTRY.SYS
BREAK=ON
FILES=30
BUFFERS=30
LASTDRIVE=E
STACKS=9,256
```

Config.sys on a 386 system running Windows 3.1 under DOS 5.0.

If your system has an 80286 processor, then leave out the command which makes reference to the 80386 memory-manager EMM386.EXE.

A brief explanation of the commands that can be included within your **config.sys** file is given on the next page. However, do remember that any changes made to this file only take effect after re-booting which can be achieved by pressing the 3 keys **Ctrl+Alt+Del** simultaneously.

Command	Function
BREAK	By including the command BREAK=ON in the **config.sys** file, you can use the key combination **Ctrl+C** (hold the key marked Ctrl down and press C) or **Ctrl+Break**, to interrupt MS-DOS I/O functions.

BUFFERS   MS-DOS allocates memory space in RAM, called buffers, to store whole sectors of data being read from disc, each of 512 bytes in size. If more data are required, MS-DOS first searches the buffers before searching the disc, which speeds up operations. The number of buffers can be changed by using:

BUFFERS=n

where n can be a number from 1 to 99.

However, as each buffer requires an additional 0.5 Kbyte of RAM, the number you should use is dependent on the relative size between the package you are using and your computer's RAM. Best results are obtained by choosing between 10-30 buffers.

COUNTRY   MS-DOS displays dates according to the US format which is month/day/year. To change this to day/month/year, use the command

COUNTRY=044

where 044 is for U.K. users.

Non U.K. users can substitute their international telephone country code for the 044. The default value is 001, for the USA.

DEVICE   MS-DOS includes its own standard device drivers which allow communication with your keyboard, screen and discs. However, these drivers can be extended to allow other devices to be connected by specifying them in the **config.sys** file. Example of these are:

DEVICE=ANSI.SYS

which loads alternative screen and keyboard drivers for ANSI support - features of which are required by some commercial software.

DEVICE=SETVER.EXE

which sets the MS-DOS version number that MS-DOS version 5 reports to a program. You can use this command at the prompt to display the version table, which lists names of programs and the number of the MS-DOS version with which they are designed to run, or add a program that has not been updated to MS-DOS 5.

DEVICE=MOUSEAnn.SYS

allows the use of specific mouse devices.

DEVICE=VDISK.SYS n

allows you to specify the size n in Kbytes (default 64) of RAM to be used as an extra very fast virtual disc. With computers which have more than 640 Kbytes of RAM, the option /E can be used after n in the command to allocate the specified memory size from the extra area of RAM.

DEVICE=DRIVER.SYS

allows you to connect an external disc drive.

DEVICE=EGA.SYS

provides mouse support for EGA modes.

DEVICE=COMn.SYS

specifies asynchronous drivers for the serial ports, where for n=01 specifies an IBM PC AT COM device, and n=02 specifies an IBM PS/2 COM device.

DEVICEHIGH Loads device drivers into the upper memory area.

DOS Sets the area of RAM where MS-DOS will be located, and specifies whether to use the upper memory area. The command takes the form:

DOS=HIGH

DRIVPARM Sets characteristics of a disc drive.

FCBS Specifies the number of FCBs that can be opened concurrently. The command takes the following form:

FCBS=x,y

where x specifies the total number of files by FCBs, from 1 to 255, that can be opened at any one time (the default value being 4), and y specifies the number of opened files (from 1-255) that cannot be closed automatically by MS-DOS if an application tries to open more than x files.

FILES MS-DOS normally allows 8 files to be opened at a time. However, some software such as relational databases, might require to refer to more files at any given time. To accommodate this, MS-DOS allows you to change this default value by using:

FILES=n

where n can be a number from 8 to the maximum required by your application which usually is 20, although the maximum allowable is 99.

INSTALL This command runs a terminate-and-stay-resident (TSR) program, such as FASTOPEN, KEYB, NLSFUNC, or SHARE while MS-DOS reads the **config.sys** file. The command takes the following form:

INSTALL=filespec[params]

where *params* specifies the optional line to pass to the *filespec* which must be FASTOPEN.EXE, KEYB.EXE, NLSFUNC.EXE or SHARE.EXE.

LASTDRIVE   This command is used if additional drives are to be connected to your system, or you are sharing a hard disc on a network. The command takes the form:

LASTDRIVE=x

where x is a letter from A to Z (default E).

REM   REM followed by any string, allows remarks to be entered in the **config.sys**.

SHELL   Manufacturers of some micros provide a 'front end' or an alternative Command Processor to COMMAND.COM as real-mode command-line processor. To invoke this, the command SHELL must be included within the **config.sys** file. The command takes the form:

SHELL=FRONTEND.COM

where FRONTEND is the name of the alternative Command Processor. The default value of SHELL is

COMMAND [options]

with the following available options:

/E   specifies the environment size in bytes, with a default value of 160 bytes

/P   prohibits COMMAND.COM from exiting to a higher level

/C   executes a following command.

STACKS   Sets the amount of RAM that MS-DOS reserves for processing hardware interrupts.

SWITCHES   Specifies the use of conventional keyboard
            functions even though an enhanced keyboard
            is installed.

The Autoexec.bat File

This is a special batch file that MS-DOS looks for during the last stages of booting up and if it exists, the commands held in it will be executed. One such command is the KEYB xx which configures keyboards for the appropriate national standard, with xx indicating the country. For the U.K., the command becomes KEYB UK, and you will need to execute it if your keyboard is marked with the double quotes sign on the 2 key and/or the @ sign over the single quotes key and/or the £ sign over the 3 key.

An example of the contents of this file are shown below for a system running Windows 3.1 under MS-DOS 5.0.

```
@ECHO OFF
SET COMSPEC=C:\DOS\COMMAND.COM
VERIFY OFF
PATH C:\WINDOWS;C:\EXCEL;C:\WINDOWS\AMIPRO;C:\DOS;C:\BATCH
LH C:\DOS\APPEND \Batch
LH C:\WINDOWS\MOUSE.COM /Y
LH C:\WINDOWS\SMARTDRV.EXE
LH C:\DOS\KEYB UK,,C:\DOS\KEYBOARD.SYS /ID:166
LH C:\DOS\GRAPHICS GRAPHICS
PROMPT $P$G
SET TEMP=D:\
ECHO H E L L O ... This your PC using
VER
```

Autoexec.bat on a 386 system running Windows 3.1 under DOS 5.0.

Do remember, that any changes made to the **autoexec.bat** file only take effect after typing **autoexec** at the system prompt, or when re-booting the system by pressing the three keys **Ctrl+Alt+Del** simultaneously.

Optimizing High Memory:
The order in which the memory-resident programs were loaded into high memory, is of some importance. The basic principle is that you load the biggest program first, then check using the

```
mem /p
```

command, to find out whether a certain memory-resident program will fit into the available 'gaps'. You might find it useful to use the |MORE pipe at the end of the MEM command to stop information from scrolling off your screen.

When MS-DOS encounters the LOADHIGH command, it attempts to load the specified program into the upper memory. However, if the program does not fit into one of the available upper memory blocks, DOS loads it into conventional memory instead. To find out where a particular program has been loaded, use the

```
mem /c |more
```

command.

Issuing this command, causes MS-DOS to display three columns of information; the first column lists the name of the program using your system's memory, the second column gives the size of the program in decimal, while the third column gives the size in hexadecimal. Both the contents of the Conventional Memory and the Upper Memory areas are listed.

If, however, you issue this command while running Windows in enhanced mode (having first shelled out to the DOS prompt before issuing the command), or if you do not include the EMM386 device driver in your **config.sys** file, then the **mem** command will not report the contents of Upper Memory.

If the name of a program or a device driver appears in the Conventional Memory area (apart from MSDOS, HIMEM, EMM386, and COMMAND), then the program or device driver is running in conventional memory, probably because it did not fit into the largest available UMB. This can happen if it is of the type that requires more memory when it is loaded than when it is running, or vice versa. Such a program or device driver might not fit into a UMB even if the size of its file is shown to be less than the largest UMB.

If programs do not load in high memory, then you might try including some additional information at the end of the line that loads the EMM386 device driver in your **config.sys** file. This could take the form:

```
i=B000-B7FF i=E000-EFFF
```

which specifically informs the EMM386 memory manager that RAM is available between pairs of addresses (expressed with the i= option). You could also ask the EMM386 memory manager to specifically exclude segments of memory, by using the x= option. However, before you do any of this, make sure that you install MS-DOS 5 on floppy discs, because if anything goes wrong, you will need a bootable disc to start up your computer.

Each machine has different regions of RAM installed between 640 Kbytes and 1024 Kbytes. For example, on genuine IBM machines, the area of memory between E000-EFFF is the Basic language ROM. Also area C000-C7FF is available, whereas on compatible machines this area is probably not available because of the addressing of various devices such as disc controller firmware. Finally, on *any* machine with a VGA display adaptor, the area of memory used by the CGA system (B000-B7FF) is available to load programs in high memory.

To manage your processor's memory in the most efficient manner, if you are not willing to experiment, you could use one of several proprietary packages which does all this for you automatically.

A list of permissible commands which you can include within the **autoexec.bat** file with a short explanation of their function is shown below:

Command	*Function*
@ECHO OFF	Turns off the echoing on the screen of commands being executed within the **autoexec.bat** file. This command remains in effect until an ECHO command with a trailing message (which is displayed on the screen) is executed.
PATH	Sets and displays the path to be searched by MS-DOS for external commands or batch files.

APPEND	Sets a path that MS-DOS will search for data files when they are not in the current directory.
VERIFY	Turns on/off verification that files are written correctly to disc.
GRAPHICS	Allows MS-DOS to print on a graphics printer the information appearing on the screen. The parameter GRAPHICS indicates that printer is either an IBM Personal Graphics Printer, an IBM Proprinter, or an IBM Quietwriter printer.
MOUSE	Loads the mouse driver that comes with the mouse device.
KEYB	Identifies the type of keyboard connected to your system.
PROMPT	Changes the appearance of the MS-DOS command prompt. The parameter $P forces the display of the current drive and path, while the parameter &G displays the greater-than sign (>).
SET	Allows an environment variable named TEMP to be associated with the string C:\WINDOWS\TEMP. This is the subdirectory where Microsoft Windows creates and later deletes temporary files.
VER	Displays the version of MS-DOS running on your system.

In the above **autoexec.bat** file, all the memory-resident programs, such as MOUSE, APPEND, etc., are loaded into high memory with the LOADHIGH command (abbreviate to LH), while the SET command is used to set the TEMP environment variable to the RAM drive D: created with the RAMDRIVE.SYS command within the **config.sys** file (the program has created this RAM drive as drive D:, because this is the first available drive letter that is not assigned to an actual drive). Setting the TEMP variable to the RAM drive, should speed up programs that require to write temporary files to disc.

INDEX

134

NOTES

138

NOTES

NOTES

NOTES

NOTES

NOTES

NOTES